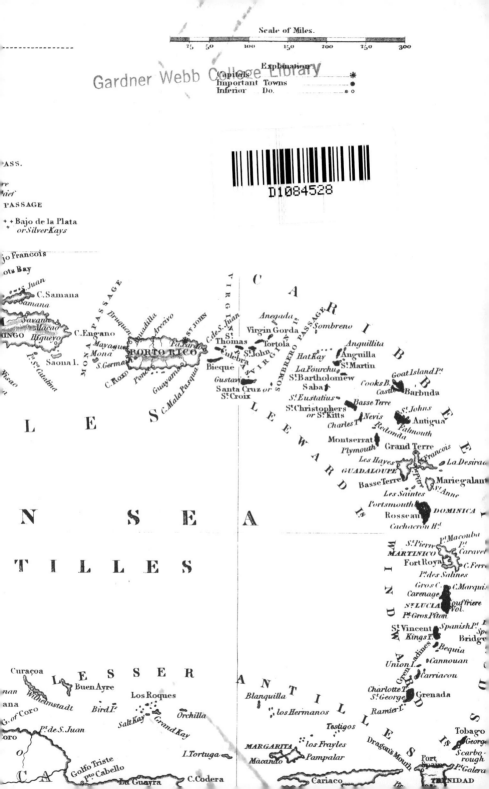

Scale of Miles.

75   50   100   150   200   250   300

Explanation

Capitals   *
Important Towns   ●
Inferior   Do.   ◦

PASS.

PASSAGE

++ Bajo de la Plata
  or SilverKays

jo François
ots Bay
C. Samana
Samana
C.S! Juan
Savane
Macao
Higuey
INGO
La S! Catalina
Saona I.
C. Engano
Mayaguez
Mona
S. German
C. Roxo
Aguadilla
Arecibo
Bruquen
PORTO RICO
Ponce
Pataxardo
Guayama
C. Mala Pasqua

VIRGIN PASSAGE
MONA PASSAGE
ST JOHN
C. de S. Juan
S!
Thomas
Culebra
Bieque
S! John
Tortola
Virgin Gorda
Anegada
Sombrero
HatKay
La Fourchu
S! Bartholomew
Saba
S! Eustatius
S! Christophers
or S! Kitts
Charles T.
Nevis
Redonda
Montserrat
Plymouth
Les Hayes
GUADALOUPE
Basse Terre
Les Saintes
Portsmouth
Rosseau
Cachacron H?

Anguillita
Anguilla
S! Martin
Cooks B.
Castl
Barbuda
Basse Terre
S! Johns
Antigua
Falmouth
Grand Terre
François
La Desirade
Mariegalante
S! Anne

Goat Island P!

DOMINICA

SOMBRERO PASSAGE
VIRGIN

C A R I B B E E
L E E W A R D Is

CARIBBEAN SEA

L E S S E R   A N T I L L E S

S. Pierre
MARTINICO
Fort Royal
P! des Salines
Gros C.
Carenage
S! LUCIA
P! Gros Piton
S! Vincent
Kings T.
Union I.
P! Macouba
P!
Caravel
C. Ferre
C. Marqui
Souffriere
Vol.
Spanish P!
Sp
Bridge
Bequia
Cannouan
Carriacou
Charlotte T.
S! George
Ramier I.
Grenada

WINDWARD Is

Curaçoa
Wilhelmstadt
G. of Coro
P! de S. Juan
oro
Golfo Triste
P? Cabello
La Guayra
C. Codera

Buen Ayre
Bird I.
Salt Kay
Grand Kay
Los Roques
Orchilla

Blanquilla
los Hermanos
Testigos
MARGARITA
Macanao
los Frayles
Pampalar
Cariaco

Tobago
George
Scarbo
rough
P! Galera
Port
TRINIDAD
Dragon's Mouth

BLACK SEPARATISM AND THE
CARIBBEAN, 1860

Black Separatism
and the Caribbean 1860

by James Theodore Holly and J. Dennis Harris

Edited, with an Introduction, by Howard H. Bell

Ann Arbor
The University of Michigan Press

EDITOR'S NOTE

I have made a serious effort to maintain the integrity of
the Harris and Holly documents. Some necessary explan-
ations occur in the introduction, some in footnotes;
others will show up here.

First, these accounts were written in the 1850's and
there are therefore differences in spelling, capitalization,
names designating specific areas, etc. The word *Negro*
was seldom capitalized until the second quarter of the
twentieth century. I have not changed the capitalization
or lack of capitalization to conform to current standards.
In 1860 the word *black* was used for color differentiation
rather than in the sense used in the late 1960's. In fact it
would be difficult to deal realistically with the history of
the island which the Spanish found under the native
name of *Hayti* (renamed *La Isla Española;* later Anglic-
ized to *Hispaniola*) without following color designation
of white, black, and mulatto as used by the "black"
authors whose works are here reproduced.

Due in part to that history, the names used for the
island and its political divisions (modern Haiti and the
Dominican Republic) are sometimes confused and possibly confusing to the reader. Harris, writing in 1860,
uses the term *Dominicana* to refer to the area and the
people of the Dominican end of the island; refers to the
country as *Santo Domingo* (but is not consistent in that
designation); and makes a point of referring to the entire
island as *San Domingo.*

Holly, perhaps in deference to the French name
Saint-Dominique for her colony wrested from Spain in
1697, calls the Haitian end of the island *St. Domingo*
almost invariably while tracing its colonial and revolu-

tionary history. With the declaration of independence in 1804 he accepts *Hayti* as the name of the country. He consistently spells the proper adjective *Haytian* while Harris spells it *Haytien* in contrast to current spelling. Either man may be guilty, in keeping with the confusion of the age, of using *Hayti, Santo Domingo* (or *San Domingo*) when referring to the entire island. This is perhaps understandable when it is recalled that Hispaniola was first under Spanish control; later divided between Spanish and French (Treaty of Ryswick, 1697); entirely under theoretical French control (Treaty of Basel, 1795); united under President Jean Pierre Boyer of Haiti for two decades; and subjected to a renewed effort at union under Faustin Élié Soulouque (Faustin I) —all by the end of the 1850's.

There is also some variation in spelling of proper names. Vincent Ogé, the leader of the mulattoes in their ill-fated bid for equality with the whites, appears in Harris as above, but is consistently spelled by Holly as *Oje; Chevanne* in Holly becomes *Chavine* in Harris.

For those acquainted with the history of the island Harris' kaleidoscopic review can be more than confusing; some of it is quite positively inaccurate. Perhaps such readers will pass quickly over his second letter where his inaccuracies are most apparent and move on to areas of description, travel, and opinion where his chief contributions lie. A few words of explanation will serve to help the average reader over a few of the highest hurdles. African slavery was introduced early in the sixteenth (not seventeenth) century; the Spanish used the Caribbean islands as springboards to continental expansion at about the same time; the French were recognized as the owners of Saint-Dominique (Haiti) in 1697 (not 1773); it is true that Dessaline's invasion of the Dominican end of the island would have put refugee French at his mercy, but Harris fails to draw a distinction between slaughtering the French and slaughtering the Spanish.

Contents

Introduction

by

HOWARD H. BELL

The decade of the 1960's witnessed the development of a black awareness and a black pride which, to the uninitiated, may seem to have erupted into full growth from the barren soil of black complacency. But nothing can be farther from the truth. The black pride of our day stands in deep debt to the Negro Nationalism of the sixth decade of the nineteenth century for its tenets. Nor were the intervening decades devoid of the elements which allowed the black community to build up the reserves which are making the current black revolution a viable experience.

Negro activists of the 1850's condemned those blacks and whites who worshiped with slaveholders; they laid intricate plans to take black problems out of white jurisdiction; they talked of frontier American communities where they would not be under white suzerainty; they insisted on equality before the law; they considered the American nation and people indebted to the black man for services rendered and for deprivation endured; they spoke of America being saved by the black man if it was to be saved at all. And there were those who would gladly have seen a revolution if it would accomplish their goals.

Finally, in the decade preceding the Civil War, a significant minority of American blacks were looking overseas for a place where Negro potential for government would have full sway, where a black nation might blossom forth, where black pride would be unimpeded.[1] The Negro's interest in emigration was intensified by a growing feeling that projects pertaining to blacks must be headed by blacks; that blacks must shoulder the full burden of their own self-betterment; that they must exercise their political potential by developing a government independent of the white man's supervision; that they must have a land "where Ethiopia might stretch forth her hand." By 1860 this new attitude, which, with some oversimplification, may be described as Negro Nationalism, was a vital force in determining action which blacks would take in the increasingly tense situation in the United States and abroad. During the decade there were projects for going to Canada or the British West Indies; there were plans for settlements in Mexico and Central America; there were efforts to create a new home in Africa. And there were those who looked to Haiti as the land of promise. Among these were James Theodore Holly, devoted to the cause of Negro Nationalism, and J. Dennis Harris, whose dedication was not as great but whose interest in establishing a nation where blacks would be in complete control seems to have been as strong in 1860 as that of other Negro activists.

It was at the National Emigration Convention at Cleveland in 1854 that Holly assumed leadership in the effort to make Haiti the center of interest for the Negro National Emigrationists. His negotiations with Haiti to open the country to Negro immigration were at first unsuccessful, but in 1858 the Haitian government issued an invitation to American blacks to make the land their future home. This encouraged a surge of interest in Haiti on the part of the emigrationists.

In May, 1859, James Redpath, journalist, abolitionist, and proven friend of the Negro, counseled caution and warned that there should be no emigration until the

President of Haiti had clarified the policy of the newly established republic.[2] Redpath was eventually accorded the position of chief agent of the Haitian Bureau of Emigration—a position which grew out of three trips which he made to the country during 1859 and 1860.[3] He stuck to the demand for guarantees to the emigrants, and these were provided in the autumn of 1860. Immigrants were promised freedom of worship, access to the land, liberal political privileges, and free passage to the island if desired.

The interest in emigration to Haiti or to any other area was an unsettling influence on the black community and therefore opposed by many. By far the most conspicuous of the anti-emigrationists was Frederick Douglass, editor of *Frederick Douglass' Paper (Douglass' Monthly* after 1860). Consistent opponent of emigration en masse, he had come close to opposing emigration for any purpose. Nevertheless when pressed, he had always recognized the right of the individual to choose his own home, and had maintained that if emigration were to take place at all, it should be to a nearby area so that the impact on the slaveholding South would be thereby intensified.

Douglass did not move readily from his anti-emigration stance, but the election of 1860 and the hectic events preceding the inauguration of a President who refused to commit himself or his party to emancipation of the slave or the uplift of the free Negro left little room for further delay in coming to grips with the problem. Douglass therefore began shifting his position. In the course of 1861 *Douglass' Monthly* regularly printed full-page advertisements of the Haitian government for American immigrants.[4] By April 1861 he had decided to visit Haiti as the guest of the Haitian government so that he could evaluate the possibilities of many American blacks making their homes in that country. He canceled his decision after the opening of the American Civil War.[5]

Perhaps Douglass was no more cautious than the great mass of American blacks, but there were those who were anxious to be on their way, and recruitment activity proceeded vigorously after receipt of the Haitian guarantees to the immigrants in the fall of 1860. Holly was among the first recruiting agents selected by Redpath. Though first assigned to lecture in the Pennsylvania-New Jersey area, his chief efforts lay in aiding the actual settlements in Haiti. John Brown, Jr., son of John Brown of Harper's Ferry fame, was to cover the Canadas, while J. Dennis Harris, only recently back from his summer on the borders of the Caribbean Sea, sought support in Ohio for the cause. Besides these, there were resident agents in New York and in Washington, D.C., and a corresponding agent for the Atlantic seaboard states.[6] Undoubtedly Douglass' near capitulation to emigrationism in April influenced others to become activists within the ranks. William J. Watkins, Douglass' chief aide in opposing Holly and other emigrationists in the middle 1850's, became a lecturer for the Haitian movement, as did William Wells Brown, another of the heretofore most articulate defenders of the stay-at-home philosophy. Along with the Reverend J. B. Smith they replaced some of the original lecturers,[7] and did yeoman work toward persuading blacks that Haiti should be their future home.

The agents went to work with a will. Harris was reported as favorably received in the Cleveland area in November, 1860.[8] In midyear, 1861, J. B. Smith, who had once been a supporter of a rival emigrationist organization, the African Civilization Society, was stumping the northern New England states and the maritime provinces of Canada. But he found little racial friction and correspondingly small tendency to emigrate. There was greater interest in the areas of the United States closer to the slave territory and in the section of Canada lying

4

between Toronto and Detroit, where most of the more recently established Negro settlements were located.

Meetings at Kalamazoo, Michigan, and at Baltimore, Maryland, accepted the philosophy that Negro progress in America was a lost cause; the people looked to Haiti as the place where ancient wrongs could be made right. In New York City the Haitian Agricultural Emigration Association was meeting every week at 127 Suffolk Street. Meanwhile from Ohio came word from J. W. Williams that a sizable group centering in Ripley was attempting to be in readiness to leave in the fall of 1861; and E. P. Walker was suggesting the desirability of using British vessels to avoid putting the emigrants at the mercy of those ships operating under letters of marque granted by the Confederacy. Walker suggested further that it would be well to send ships to the ports of the Great Lakes so that emigrants could be spared the tiring rail journey to Atlantic loading stations.[9]

Possibly the most enthusiastic reports came from J. B. Smith who was, by the summer of 1861, working in Pennsylvania. He held that "The people are tired of living on promises based upon groundless imaginations and forlorn hopes." Then, putting words into the mouths of his listeners, he stated their position: "Don't tell me to wait a century for the accomplishment of a thing here that I may more effectually do in a score of years somewhere else. We are tired of being led by the blind, and have concluded to change our policy."[10] Smith was especially enthusiastic about his reception at Lewistown, Pittsburgh, and York. At Lewistown he found a company drilling in military tactics, determined to go to Haiti despite the military unrest on the island occasioned by the Spanish designs on Santo Domingo.[11]

Meantime, California, which had a Negro population of about five thousand,[12] gave a ready ear to the idea of a Negro nation centered in Haiti. In June, 1861 there was an inquiry from Thomas Taylor of San Francisco about the emigration program. Taylor stated that many people there were interested in going. Redpath thereupon recommended to the Haitian Government that Holly be sent there to open an agency.[13] Two months later Dr. W. H. C. Stephenson was writing from Sacramento, corroborating Taylor's statements, and urging that the Haitian Government provide transportation for those who would like to emigrate.[14] There seems, however, to have been no agency established, for as late as November Dr. Stephenson was still asking for one and insisting that people in Marysville, Sacramento, Ploverville, and other places were anxious for a chance to join the march to Haiti.[15]

The majority of Negro communities in Canada, like those in California, were composed of settlers only recently arrived. In Canada, however, in striking contrast to the situation on the West Coast, the immigrants were in territory close to the bulk of the Negro population in the Northern states. Physical location, then, may account in large part for the failure of the Haitian authorities to encourage the Californians, while from the very first the Canadians were courted with particular care.

During the first six months of 1861 some seven groups had been sent on their way to Haiti.[16] By that time there was a Rochester Colony and a New Haven Colony, and probably others named after American cities. In April, however, the Civil War in the United States had begun, and in May the Spanish had moved to take over the Dominican end of Hispaniola.[17] Although the Civil War in the United States made no immediate physical demands on the colored people, the threat of military action at the other end of the line could not fail to be a disturbing factor.[18]

Under these circumstances Redpath felt it necessary to suspend emigration for two months while war appeared likely to develop between Haiti and Spain.[19]

There was, however, some feeling that colonization should not be suspended merely because of physical danger. John W. Stokes, writing from Toronto, contended that the Spanish trouble should be an incentive to emigration, rather than a deterrent. He envisaged colored people of the United States and Canada as flocking to Haiti to defend the Negro nation against the Spanish. Furthermore, with Haiti delivered from such a threat, Porto Rico and Cuba could be added to the free Negro group in the Caribbean, and slaveholding Spain thus discomfited.[20]

When the ban was lifted the movement was resumed with some vigor, and enthusiasm in some areas seemed to be continuing. Nevertheless, the Haitian emigration movement was on the defensive from the first of the year, 1862. Reports began to filter back from the island that many of the emigrants were unhappy with conditions in what they had believed to be a land of promise. Haiti's need was not for hairdressers, unattached women, the aged, or caterers. Only those accustomed to a farming life, and preferably those already familiar with problems of the frontier, were welcome as immigrants.[21] Some of the unwanted classes slipped through, and once there were in a good position to become disaffected if things did not work as they had unreasonably hoped they would. Furthermore, the Haitian government seems to have been unable to do as much for the immigrants as it had promised.

Sickness and death, due in part to unavoidable problems connected with resettlement, became a severe detriment to the program as time passed. John W. Stokes, who had hoped to help redeem the Caribbean, had died there by January of 1862. A few months later deaths in the St. Marks area reached such proportions that an official investigation was made. It was claimed that chief reasons for the heavy mortality were lack of cleanliness, excesses in eating and drinking, and a smallpox epidemic which had been introduced by one of the immigrant parties. Regardless of where the fault lay, the record discouraged those who had considered emigrating.[22]

Just how many emigrated to Haiti, or how many remained, is uncertain. One report indicated that two thousand English-speaking immigrants were located within a ten-mile radius of St. Marks at the end of the year, 1861.[22] These were not necessarily all from the United States and Canada, but might include immigrants from British Caribbean dependencies. Several months later there was an estimate that some twelve hundred to fourteen hundred "Afric-Americans" were living in the St. Marks area, and other established settlements were noted, but the number of American immigrants was not listed.[23] A man closely associated with the movement from start to finish was later to make the claim that a total of about two thousand went out, and that about one-third of them remained.[24]

When all factors are considered, the odds against emigration were too great. Hope of a Union victory in America, failure to find conditions in Haiti as favorable as had been anticipated, diversion of the interest of some would-be emigrationists to other emigration projects, criticism from disaffected groups—all played a hand in the failure of Haitian emigration. One careful observer of the Haitian scene stated that emigration "failed because there was neither enterprise nor capital, awaiting the emigrants in Haiti, by which alone the poor and ignorant, on arrival in a new country, can be enabled to work with success.[25]

By the end of 1862, Zion Church in New York City was welcoming some of the returning emigrationists and they organized at that time an Anti-Emigration League to give succor to those returning, and to advise others to stay in the United States.[26]

The authors of the works presented in this volume, James Theodore Holly and J. Dennis Harris, differed in their basic goals, as will become evident in reading their respective accounts, but they shared the central hope of supporting a viable black government which would be a rallying point for black pride and black achievement. This government would at the same time serve the purpose of bringing American slavery and the degredation of the free Negro to an end, not only by competing with the economy of the American South, but also by providing a place of refuge for escaping slaves.

Holly was born in 1829 just as radical antislavery sentiment and action (David Walker, Nat Turner, William Lloyd Garrison) were getting under way. Securing what education was open to him in the nation's capital, and later in New York, Buffalo, and Detroit, young Holly developed an early interest in the plight of the people from whom a part of his physical heritage had come. Unlike the majority of his contemporaries, he saw the future of the black race, not in America, but in some locality removed from the presence of the whites. And unlike many idealists of that day and this, Holly remained true to his convictions throughout a long life of service to mankind.

Holly had learned the shoemaker's trade from his father but his other interests left little time for making a livelihood at that vocation. When he was scarcely twenty-one he approached the American Colonization Society with the suggestion that he be trained in some medically related profession with a view to emigration to Liberia. A year later he participated in a convention at Toronto which called upon the American Negro to look to Canada and the British West Indies as future homes. Thereafter for a time he served as associate editor of Henry Bibb's Canadian-based *Voice of the Fugitive* which appealed constantly to American Negroes to come to Canada.

Holly was thus early identified with emigrationism and the Negro Nationalism which was inextricably interwoven with that philosophy, but he did not have a closed mind on where the future of the black man lay. He had looked with favor on both Canada and the British West Indies, but by 1854 he had become interested in Haiti, an interest which may have developed along with his interest in the Protestant Episcopal Church. An active participant in the National Emigration Convention at Cleveland in 1854 and newly ordained deacon in the Episcopal Church in 1855, Holly visited Haiti in 1855 to determine the practicability of American black emigration. In 1857 he wrote his *Vindication*. In 1861, now an Episcopal priest, he ended his lecturing activities in the United States and emigrated to Haiti.

Holly's own words may serve to explain the depth of feeling which could drive a man to forsake his homeland and cast his lot with the inhabitants of a country with less potential in almost every area normally considered as essential to security and comfort. Recalling that great progress had been made in humanitarian projects in the nineteenth century, he yet saw most Caucasians as arrogating to themselves the higher virtues while excluding the Negro. Even the "noisy agitators of the present day . . . have lurking in their heart of hearts, a secret infidelity in regard to the real equality of the black man."[27] And if there were those who did recognize full equality, they failed to stand up and be counted. Faced with overwhelming sentiment of inequality in America, the black man actually lost confidence in himself. "And the result is, that many of the race themselves, are almost persuaded that they are a brood of inferior beings."[28]

Holly sees in the history of Haiti a chance to revive the black man's confidence in himself, a confidence stolen from him during three hundred years of enslavement, but now gloriously reestablished among the Haitian people through a revolution accomplished against the greatest odds, and the subsequent establishment and continuation of a viable government. Despite great disappointment, personal tragedy, and the failure of the emigration project, he stayed on in his adopted country. In 1874 he was consecrated Episcopal Bishop of Haiti, and to the end of his life he remained loyal to his Christian mission and to his confidence in the eventual success of a proud black nation.

J. Dennis Harris shared with Holly his belief in the efficacy of an Anglo-African nation in the Caribbean area, but Harris' interests tended to the economic and the opportunistic rather than to the philosophical and the idealistic. He had not served a lengthy apprenticeship in the organized efforts to improve the lot of the black man in America as Holly and many others had done. He shows up in 1858 in a letter to Congressman Frank P. Blair, Jr., expressing an interest in Blair's scheme for colonizing free blacks in Central America; he attends the "Convention of Colored Men of Ohio" the same year; he is soon involved in a "Central American Land Company" project; and by 1860 is embarked on his trip into the Caribbean.

A Summer on the Borders of the Caribbean Sea, published in that same year, consists of letters written by Harris in the course of his trip. In various places he implies that his letters are to be published serially. It will be noted also that his chapter titles are listed as Letter I, Letter II, etc. In the early part of Letter IX, after referring to James Redpath's letters to the *Tribune* [New York] on Haiti and some of the inadequacies of those letters, he states "be it mine and the *Anglo-African's* [*The Weekly Anglo-African* of New York] to undertake what the *Tribune* and its correspondent failed to supply." Letter I, as it appears in *A Summer on the Borders of the Caribbean Sea,* complete with note at the end of the chapter, was printed in *The Weekly Anglo-African* for July 14, 1860. It was signed "H," a designation which Harris used in his letters when referring to himself. Further proof that the letters were all published in *The Weekly Anglo-African* must await new discoveries of the succeeding issues of that excellent weekly, for July 14 was the last extant issue until sometime in the following year.

Since a substantial portion of Harris's recital deals with the history of Santo Domingo and Haiti, and since he wrote as hurriedly as he did, he resorted to copying extensively from extant works and thereby becomes the reflector of the opinions of the authors selected, except as he notes his own viewpoints in asides or evaluations. On the whole he is careful to indicate the sources he uses, but is not to be hampered by extensive footnotes. On page seventy-seven he states that "The following compilation will be taken from Rainsford's, St. Domingo, and Edwards' and Coke's histories of the West Indies, but principally, and when not otherwise marked, from Coke." Bryan Edwards' *The History, Civil and Commercial, of the British West Indies . . . With a Continuation to the Present Time* (5th ed.; 5 vols.; London: G. and W. B. Whittaker, 1818–19) includes a historical survey of Santo Domingo. Marcus Rainsford wrote *A Memoir of the Transactions That Took Place in St. Domingo, in the Spring of 1799; . . .* (London: Printed by R. B. Scott, 1802), while Thomas Coke contributed a Methodist Mission-oriented *A History of the West Indies . . . .* (3 vols.; Liverpool: Printed by Nuttall, Fisher, and Dixon, 1808–11).

Other authors, including Anthony Trollope, Ephraim George Squier, Herman Burmeister, William Vincent Wells, Moreau de Saint-Méry, and Wilshire S. Courtney, are cited or referred to, and where it seems appropriate bibliographical information has been added in notes at the bottom of the pages.

Harris is at his best in recounting his own experiences or in repeating the stories or snatches of conversation which come to him as he takes his leisurely way through the islands. Here he exposes his own feelings

of black yankee superiority over the natives; his love of
the natural beauty of the islands; his quick eye for improving roads, ports, agriculture, industry, his equally
quick eye for the beauty of the fairer sex. Here too his
ironic comments or asides enliven an already interesting
account. He describes his stay with the Pastorisas, then
suddenly remembers that he should call attention to
Señora Pastorisa's being "slightly tinged"—the handsomest woman in the world."[29] He wonders why William
Whipper, a black Philadelphia merchant, should devote
his money to running a steamboat up a Canadian creek
to aid black emigrants there when he could accomplish
the same beneficent purpose—and make infinitely more
money in the process on a similar business venture in
the vast seaways of the Caribbean—"The tenacity with
which our leading colored men embrace that short-
sighted policy which teaches them to confine their enterprises to certain proscribed [prescribed?] prejudice-cursed
districts, is not only extraordinary—it is marvellous."[30]

At one time or another Harris pays his respects to
William Walker, the American filibusterer; to Hinton
Rowan Helper, the expatriate Southerner who, while
opposing slavery, wanted to send all blacks "back to
Africa"; to an unidentified Mr. Corwin who "may
thank Heaven if he is not yet arrested as a fugitive
slave."[31] This gibe may well be an example of the
Negro's reminder to some whites that their bloodstream
stemmed not entirely from the Caucasian.

Harris is surprisingly nonpartisan when reciting
the bestialities of the Haitian Revolution. In fact the
reader is very likely to get the impression that the author
is watching the drama unfold from a distance; that he is
deriving a certain ironic satisfaction from the spectacle;
that he is not particularly interested in who is doing
what to whom. He starts from the premise that whites
are going to hold onto whatever advantage they have,
at whatever cost in blood and tears, especially the blood

and tears of the blacks. But having dealt with the whites, he catalogues, with something bordering on sardonic humor, the worst from the blacks and the mulattoes.

This seeming ambivalence is perhaps more characteristic of Harris than of any of the other Negro writers of the era. Certainly it is not to be found in the writings of those with the deep dedication of Holly. Nevertheless, Holly and most other American blacks of this era shared with Harris in one degree or another the concept that they were to play the role of the black yankee, and that they carried the key to heaven on earth and in heaven. Holly weeps for a downtrodden people and works for the uplift of all blacks; Harris notes their lowly position with a certain air of detachment. Always a yankee, but always aware of his African heritage, he sees the American tropics as a land where black American ingenuity and the Afro-European blood and culture combine to serve the best interests of the area. He sees the "infusion of Northern blood as one of the means by which the more sluggish race of the tropics is to be quickened and given energy."[32] But to Harris, the American tropics was never to be the land of the white man! Significantly perhaps, he stops short of claiming that the area would be the land of the African; rather, it would be the land where African and European blood mingled to produce a new people and a new culture. He would call this new culture the Anglo-African. He predicts for the Anglo-Africans, and here he would have been joined by Holly, that they would set themselves the goal of the creation of an independent position, "an empire which shall challenge the admiration of the world, rivalling the glory of their historic ancestors, whose undying fame was chronicled by the everlasting pyramids at the dawn of civilization."[33]

Notes to the Introduction

1. See the editor's "The Negro Emigration Movement, 1849–1854: A Phase of Negro Nationalism," *Phylon,* XX (Summer, 1959), pp. 132–142, and his "American Negro Interest in Africa, 1858–1861," *The Journal of Social Science Teachers,* VI (November, 1960), pp. 11–18.

2. *Douglass' Monthly,* May 1859, p. 78. In 1859 Haiti overthrew Faustin I and installed Fabre Geffrard as president of the republic (1859–1867). Douglass, an escaped slave, edited and published his own newspaper under varying titles between 1847 and 1863. During the 1850s he was perhaps the most universally respected of American Negro leaders.

3. James Redpath, ed., *A Guide to Hayti* (Boston: Thayer & Eldridge, 1860), pp. [9]–11.

4. Howard H. Bell, "A Survey of the Negro Convention Movement, 1830–1861" (Unpublished Ph.D. dissertation, Department of History, Northwestern University), pp. 217–222. Hereafter cited as Bell, "Negro Convention Movement."

5. *Douglass' Monthly,* May, 1861, pp. [449]–450.

6. *Ibid.,* January, 1861, p. 399.

7. *The Pine and Palm,* June 8, 1861; September 21, 1861. Watkins had been a bitter opponent of Negro emigration when associated with *Frederick Douglass' Paper* in the mid-1850s. Brown, equally opposed to emigration until the eve of the Civil War, had been a loyal follower of William Lloyd Garrison and the radical abolitionists.

8. *Cleveland Morning Leader,* November 22, 1860.

9. Bell, "Negro Convention Movement," p. 250.

10. *The Pine and Palm,* August 3, 1861.

11. *Ibid.* 1861 Santo Domingo surrendered its sovereignty to Spain, and Haiti did not take kindly to the arrangement. For a time it appeared that there would be war.

12. *Proceedings of the First State Convention of the Colored Citizens of the State of California. Held at Sacramento Nov/ember/ 20th/ ,/ 21st, and 22nd, in the Colored Methodist Church* (Sacramento: *Democratic State Journal,* 1855), p. 18.

13. *The Pine and Palm,* June 8, 1861.
14. *Ibid.,* August 17, 1861. Perhaps one reason for the urgency was that gold was no longer so plentiful in 1860, and many people were ready to try their fortunes elsewhere.
15. *Ibid.,* November 16, 1861.
16. *Cleveland Morning Leader,* June 24, 1861.
17. *The Pine and Palm,* May 25, 1861.
18. *The British and Foreign Anti-Slavery Reporter,* July 1, 1861, p. 147; *Cleveland Morning Leader,* June 24, 1861.
19. *The Pine and Palm,* July 20, 1861.
20. *Ibid.,* July 6, 1861.
21. *Ibid.,* May 1, 1862.
22. *Ibid.,* May 29, 1862.
23. *Ibid.,* December 28, 1861; July 3, 1862.
24. John W. Cromwell, *The Negro in American History: Men and Women Eminent in the Evolution of the American of African Descent* (Washington: The American Negro Academy, 1914), p. 44.
25. Benjamin P. Hunt, [Annotated bibliography in manuscript on West Indian material in his collection—no title given], in Benjamin P. Hunt Collection, Boston Public Library.
26. *The Liberator,* June 12, 1863.
27. Ja[me]s Theo[dore] Holly, *A Vindication of the Capacity of the Negro Race for Self-Government, and Civilized Progress, as Demonstrated by Historical Events of the Haytian Revolution; and the Subsequent Acts of that People Since Their National Independence* (New Haven: Published for the Afric-American Printing Co., by William H. Stanley, 1857), pp. 4–5.
28. *Ibid.,* p. 5.
29. J Dennis Harris, *A Summer on the Borders of the Caribbean Sea* (New York: A. B. Burdick, 1860), p. 41.
30. *Ibid.,* p. 136.
31. *Ibid.,* p. 35.
32. *Ibid.,* p. 139.
33. *Ibid.,* p. 176.

A

VINDICATION

OF THE

CAPACITY

OF THE NEGRO RACE

FOR

Self-Government, and Civilized Progress,

AS

DEMONSTRATED BY HISTORICAL EVENTS

OF THE

HAYTIAN REVOLUTION;

AND THE

SUBSEQUENT ACTS OF THAT PEOPLE
SINCE THEIR NATIONAL INDEPENDENCE.

A LECTURE
BY REV. JAS. THEO. HOLLY

DEDICATION

TO REV. WILLIAM C. MUNROE,

Rector of St. Matthew's Church, Detroit, Michigan

R E V . A N D D E A R S I R :—Permit me the honor of inscribing
this work to you. It is a lecture that I prepared and delivered
before a Literary Society of Colored Young Men, in the City
of New Haven, Ct., after my return from Hayti, in the autumn
of 1855; and subsequently repeated in Ohio, Michigan, and
Canada West, during the summer of 1856.

I have permitted it to be published at the request of the
Afric-American Printing Company, an association for the
publication of negro literature, organized in connection with
the Board of Publication, which forms a constituent part of
the National Emigration Convention, over which you so ably
presided, at its sessions, held in Cleveland, Ohio, in the years
1854–6.

I dedicate this work to you, in token of my appreciation
of the life-long services you have so sacredly devoted to the
cause of our oppressed race; the ardor of which devotion has
not yet abated, although the evening of your life has far ad-
vanced in the deepening shadows of the approaching night of
physical death.

And as the ground-work of this skeleton treatise is based
in the events of Haytian History, it becomes peculiarly appropriate that I should thus dedicate it to one who has spent
three of the most valuable years of his life as a missionary of
the cross in that island; who there deposited the slumbering
ashes of his own bosom companion a willing sacrifice to her
constancy and devotion; and who yet desires to consume the
remainder of his own flickering lamp of life by the resumption
of those labors in that island, under more favorable and better
auspices, in the service of Christ and his church.

Finally, I dedicate this work to you as a filial token of

gratitude, for that guidance which under God, I have received from your fatherly teachings; by which I have been awakened to higher inspirations, of our most holy religion; aroused to deeper emotions of human liberty and quicker pulsations of the universal brotherhood of man; and thereby animated with a more consecrated devotion to the service of my suffering race than might otherwise have fallen to my lot.

Deign, therefore, I beseech you, to accept this dedication as the spontaneous offering of a grateful and dutiful heart.

I have the honor to remain,
Rev. and Dear Sir,
Your most Devoted Friend and Servant,
In the cause of God and Humanity.
JAMES THEODORE HOLLY, *Rector of St. Luke's Church*
New Haven, Conn., August 1st, 1857.

Lecture

The task that I propose to myself in the present lecture, is an earnest attempt to defend the inherent capabilities of the negro race, for self-government and civilized progress. For this purpose, I will examine the events of Haytian History, from the commencement of their revolution down to the present period, so far as the same may contribute to illustrate the points I propose to prove and defend. Permit me, however, to add, in extenuation of this last comprehensive proposition, that I must, necessarily, review these events hastily, in order to crowd them within the compass of an ordinary lecture.

REASONS FOR ASSUMING SUCH A TASK

Notwithstanding the remarkable progress of philanthropic ideas and humanitarian feelings, during the last half century, among almost every nation and people throughout the habitable globe; yet the great mass of the Caucasian race still deem the negro as entirely destitute of those qualities, on which they selfishly predicate their own superiority.

And we may add to this overwhelming class that cherish such self-complacent ideas of themselves, to the great prejudice of the negro, a large quota also of that small portion of the white race, who profess to believe the truths, "That God is no respector of persons;" and that "He has made of one blood, all the nations that dwell upon the face of the earth." Yes, I say, we may add a large number of the noisy agitators of the present day, who would persuade themselves and the world, that they are really christian philanthropists, to that overwhelming crowd who openly traduce the negro; because too many of those pseudo-humanitarians have lurking in their heart of hearts, a secret infidelity in regard to the real equality of the black man, which is ever ready to manifest its concealed sting, when the full and unequivocal recognition of the negro, in all respects, is pressed home upon their hearts.

Hence, between this downright prejudice against this long abused race, which is flauntingly maintained by myriads of their oppressors on the one hand; and this woeful distrust of his natural equality, among those who claim to be his friends, on the other; no earnest and fearless efforts are put forth to vindicate their character, by even the few who may really acknowledge this equality of the races. They are overawed by the overpowering influence of the contrary sentiment. This sentiment unnerves their hands and palsies their tongue; and no pen is wielded or voice heard, among that race of men, which fearlessly and boldly places the negro side by side with the white man, as his equal in all respects. But to the contrary, every thing is done by the enemies of the negro race to vilify and debase them. And the result is, that many of the race themselves, are almost persuaded that they are a brood of inferior beings.

It is then, to attempt a fearless but truthful vindication of this race, with which I am identified—however feeble and immature that effort may be—that I now proceed to set forth the following address:

I wish, by the undoubted facts of history, to cast back the vile aspersions and foul calumnies that have been heaped upon my race for the last four centuries, by our unprincipled oppressors; whose base interest, at the expense of our blood and our bones, have made them reiterate, from generation to generation, during the long march of ages, every thing that would prop up the impious dogma of our natural and inherent inferiority.

AN ADDITIONAL REASON FOR THE PRESENT TASK

But this is not all. I wish hereby to contribute my influence—however small that influence—to effect a grandeur and dearer object to our race than even this truthful vindication of them before the world. I wish to do all in my power to inflame the latent embers of self-respect, that the cruelty and injustice of our oppressors, have nearly extinguished in our bosoms, during the midnight chill of centuries, that we have clanked the galling chains of slavery. To this end, I wish to remind my oppressed brethren, that dark and dismal as this horrid night has been, and sorrowful as the general reflections are, in regard to our race; yet, notwithstanding these discouraging considerations, there are still some proud historic recollections, linked indissolubly with the most important events of the past and present century, which break the general monotony, and remove some of the gloom that hang[s] over the dark historic period of African slavery, and the accursed traffic in which it was cradled.

THE REVOLUTIONARY HISTORY OF HAYTI

THE BASIS OF THIS ARGUMENT

These recollections are to be found in the history of the heroic events of the Revolution of Hayti.

This revolution is one of the noblest, grandest, and most justifiable outbursts against tyrannical oppression that is recorded on the pages of the world's history.

A race of almost dehumanized men—made so by an oppressive slavery of three centuries—arose from their slumber of ages, and redressed their own unparalleled wrongs with a terrible hand in the name of God and humanity.

In this terrible struggle for liberty, the Lord of Hosts

directed their arms to be the instruments of His judgment on their oppressors, as the recompense of His violated law of love between man and his fellow, which these tyrants of the new world had been guilty of, in the centuries of blood, wrong, and oppression, which they had perpetrated on the negro race in that isle of the Caribbean Sea.

But aside from this great providential and religious view of this great movement, that we are always bound to seek for, in all human affairs, to see how they square with the mind of God, more especially if they relate to the destinies of nations and people;—the Haytian Revolution is also the grandest political event of this or any other age. In weighty causes, and wondrous and momentous features, it surpasses the American revolution, in an incomparable degree. The revolution of this country was only the revolt of a people already comparatively free, independent, and highly enlightened. Their greatest grievance was the imposition of three pence per pound tax on tea, by the mother country, without their consent. But the Haytian revolution was a revolt of an uneducated and menial class of slaves, against their tyrannical oppressors, who not only imposed an absolute tax on their unrequited labor, but also usurped their very bodies; and who would have been prompted by the brazen infidelity of the age then rampant, to dispute with the Almighty, the possession of the souls of these poor creatures, could such brazen effrontery have been of any avail, to have wrung more ill-gotten gain out of their victims to add to their worldly goods.

These oppressors, against whom the negro insurgents of Hayti had to contend, were not only the government of a far distant mother country, as in the case of the American revolution; but unlike and more fearful than this revolt, the colonial government of Hayti was also thrown in the balance against the negro revolters. The American revolters had their colonial government in their own hands, as well as their individual liberty at the commencement of the revolution. The black insurgents of Hayti had yet to grasp both their personal liberty and the control of their colonial government, by the might of their own right hands, when their heroic struggle began.

The obstacles to surmount, and the difficulties to contend against, in the American revolution, when compared to those of the Haytian, were, (to use a homely but classic phrase,) but a "tempest in a teapot," compared to the dark and lurid thunder storm of the dissolving heavens.

Never before, in all the annals of the world's history, did a nation of abject and chattel slaves arise in the terrific might of their resuscitated manhood, and regenerate, redeem, and disenthrall themselves: by taking their station at one gigantic bound, as an independent nation, among the sovereignties of the world.

It is, therefore, the unparalleled incidents that led to this wonderful event, that I now intend to review rapidly, in order to demonstrate thereby, the capacity of the negro race for self-government and civilized progress, to the fullest extent and in the highest sense of these terms.

PRELIMINARY INCIDENTS OF THE REVOLUTION

I shall proceed to develop the first evidence of the competency of the negro race for self-government, amid the historical incidents that preceded their terrible and bloody revolution; and in the events of that heroic struggle itself.

When the cosmopolitan ideas of "Liberty, Fraternity, and Equality," which swayed the mighty minds of France, toward the close of the 18th century, reached the colony of St. Domingo, through the Massaic club, composed of wealthy colonial planters, organized in the

French capitol; all classes in that island, except the black slave and the free colored man, were instantly wrought up to the greatest effervescence, and swayed with the deepest emotions, by the startling doctrines of the equal political rights of all men, which were then so boldly enunciated in the face of the tyrannical despotisms and the immemorial assumptions of the feudal aristocracies of the old world.

The colonial dignitaries, the military officers, and other agents of the government of France, then resident in St. Domingo, the rich planters and the poor whites, (these latter called in the parlance of that colony *"Les petits blancs,)* were all from first to last, swayed with the intensest and the most indescribable feelings, at the promulgation of these bold and radical theories.

All were in a perfect fever to realize and enjoy the priceless boon of political and social privileges that these revolutionary ideas held out before them. And in their impatience to grasp these precious prerogatives, they momentarily forgot their colonial dependance on France, and spontaneously came together in a general assembly, at a small town of St. Domingo, called St. Marc; and proceeded to deliberate seriously about taking upon themselves all the attributes of national sovereignty and independence.

And when they had deliberately matured plans to suit themselves, they did not hesitate to send representatives to propose them to the national government of France, for its acknowledgment and acquiescence in their desires.

Such was the radical consequence to which the various classes of white colonists in St. Domingo seized upon, and carried the cosmopolitan theories of the French philosophers and political agitators of the last century.

But from all this excitement and enthusiasm, I have already excepted the black and colored inhabitants of that island.

The white colonists of St. Domingo, like our *liberty loving* and *democratic* fellow citizens of the United States, never meant to include this despised race, in their glowing dreams of "Liberty, Equality, and Fraternity."

Like our *Model Republicans,* they looked upon this hated race of beings, as placed so far down the scale of humanity, that when the "Rights of man" were spoken of, they did not imagine that the most distant reference was thereby made to the negro; or any one through whose veins his tainted blood sent its crimsoned tide.

And so blind were they to the fact that the "Rights of Man" could be so construed as to recognise the humanity of that oppressed race; that when the National assembly of France, swayed by the just representations of the "Friends of the Blacks" was led to extend equal political rights to the free men of color in St. Domingo, at the same time that this National body ratified the doings of the General Colonial assembly of St. Marc: these same colonists who had been so loud in their hurrahs for the *Rights of Man,* now ceased their clamors for liberty in the face of this just national decree, and sullenly resolved "To die rather than share equal political rights with a bastard race." Such was the insulting term that this colonial assembly then applied to the free men of color, in whose veins coursed the blood of the proud planter, commingled with that of the lowly negress.

THE SELF-POSSESSION OF THE BLACKS

AN EVIDENCE OF THEIR CAPACITY FOR SELF-GOVERNMENT
The exceptional part which the blacks played in the moving drama that was then being enacted in St. Domingo, by their stern self-possession amid the furious excitement of the whites, is one of the strongest proofs that can be adduced to substantiate the capabilities of the negro race for self-government.

The *careless reserve* of the seemingly dehumanized black slave, who continued to toil and delve on, in the monotonous round of plantation labor, under a cruel task master, in a manner so entirely heedless of the furious hurrahs for freedom and independence; the planting of Liberty poles, surmounted by the cap of Liberty; and the erection of statues to the goddess of Liberty, which was going on around him: this apparent indifference and carelessness to the surging waves of freedom that were then awakening the despotisms of earth from their slumber of ages, showed that the slave understood and appreciated the difficulties of his position. He felt that the hour of destiny, appointed by the Almighty, had not yet tolled its summons for him to arise, and avenge the wrong of ages.

He therefore remained heedless of the effervescence of liberty that bubbled over in the bosom of the white man; and continued at his sullen labors, biding his time for deliverance. And in this judicious reserve on the part of the blacks, we have one of the strongest traits of self-government.

When we look upon this characteristic of cool self-possession, we cannot but regard it as almost a miracle under the circumstances. We cannot see what magic power could keep such a warm blooded race of men in such an ice bound spell of cold indifference, when every other class of men in that colony was flush with the excitement of *liberty;* and the whole island was rocked to its center, with the deafening surges of EQUALITY, that echoed from ten thousand throats.

One would have supposed, that at the very first sound of freedom, the 500,000 bondmen in that island, whose ancestry for three centuries had worn the yoke of slavery; would have raised up, at once, in their overwhelming numerical power and physical stalwartness, and cried out LIBERTY! with a voice so powerful as to have cleft asunder the bowels of the earth, and buried slavery and every negro hater and oppressor who might dare oppose their just rights, in one common grave.

But as I have said, they did no such thing; they had a conscious faith in the ultimate designs of God; and they silently waited, trusting to the workings of His over-ruling Providence to bring about the final day of their deliverance. In doing so, I claim they have given an evidence of their ability to govern themselves, that ought to silence all proslavery calumniators of my race at once, and forever, by its powerful and undying refutation of their slanders.

And let no one dare to rob them of this glorious trait of character, either by alleging that they remained thus indifferent, because they were too ignorant to appreciate the blessings of liberty; or by saying, that if they understood the import of these clamors for the "Rights of Man," they were thus quiet, because they were too cowardly to strike for their disenthralment.

The charge that they were thus ignorant of the priceless boon of freedom, is *refuted* by the antecedent history of the servile insurrections, which never ceased to rack that island from 1522 down to the era of negro independence. The negro insurgents, Polydore, Macandel, and Padrejan, who had at various times, led on their enslaved brethren to daring deeds, in order to regain their God-given liberty, brand that assertion as a libel on the negro character, that says, he was too cowardly to strike for the inheritance of its precious boon.

And the desperate resolution to be free, that the Maroon negroes of the island maintained for 85 years, by their valorous struggles, in their wild mountain fastnesses, against the concentrated and combined operations of the French and Spanish authorities then in that colony; and which finally compelled these authorities to conclude a treaty with the intrepid Maroon chief, Santiago, and thereby acknowledge their freedom forever thereafter: this fact, I say, proves him to be a base calumniator, who shall dare to say that a keen appreciation of liberty existed not in the bosom of the negroes of St. Domingo.

But again, as to the plea of cowardice, in order to account for the fact of their cool self-possession amidst the first convulsive throes of Revolutionary liberty, permit me to add in refutation of this fallacy, that if the daring incidents of antecedent insurrections do not sufficiently refute this correlative charge also; then the daring deeds of dreadless heroism performed by a Toussaint, a Dessalines, a Rigaud, and a Christophe, in the subsequent terrible, but necessary revolution of the negroes; in which black troops gathered from the plantations of slavery, met the best appointed armies of France, and at various times, those of England and Spain also: and proved their equal valor and prowess with these best disciplined armies of Europe—this dreadless heroism, evinced by the blacks, I say, is sufficient to nail the infamous imputation of cowardice to the wall, at once and forever.

Hence nothing shall rob them of the immaculate glory of exhibiting a stern self-possession, in that feverish hour of excitement, when every body around them were crying out Liberty. And in this judicious self-control at this critical juncture, when their destiny hung on the decision of the hour, we have a brilliant illustration of the capacity of the race for self-government.

SIMILAR EVIDENCE ON THE PART OF THE FREE MEN OF COLOR

But additional and still stronger evidence of this fact crowds upon us, when we see that the free men of color remained entirely passive during the first stage of this revolutionary effervescence. This class of men, as a general thing, was educated and wealthy; and they were burthened with duties by the State, without being invested with corresponding political privileges. From such unjust exactions they had every reason to seek a speedy deliverance. And this great tumult that now swept over the island, offered them a propitious opportunity to agitate with the rest of the free men of the colony for the removal of their political disabilities.

They had greater cause to agitate than the whites, because they suffered under heavier burdens than that class. Nevertheless, in the first great outbreak of the water-floods of liberty—tempting as the occasion was, and difficult as restraint must have been; yet the free men of color also possessed their souls in patience, and awaited a more propitious opportunity. Certainly no one will attempt to stigmatise the calm judgment of these men in this awful crisis of suspense, as the result of ignorance of the blessings of freedom, when it is known that many of this class were educated in the seminaries of France, under her most brilliant professors; and that they were also patrons of that prodigy of literature, the Encyclopedia of France.

Neither can they stigmatize this class of men as cowards, as it is also known that they were the voluntary compeers of the Revolutionary heroes of the United States; and who, under the banners of France, mingled their sable blood with the Saxon and the French in the heroic battle of Savannah.

Then this calm indifference of the men of color in this crisis, notwithstanding the blood of three excitable races mingled in their veins with that of the African, viz: that of the French, the Spanish, and the Indian; and notwithstanding, they had glorious recollections of their services in the cause of American Independence, inciting them on—this calm indifference, on their part, I say, notwithstanding these exciting causes, is another grand and striking illustration of the conservative characteristics of the negro race, that demonstrate their capacity for self-government.

THE OPPORTUNE MOVEMENT OF THE FREE COLORED MEN

The tumultuous events of this excitement among the white colonists rolled onward, and brought the auspicious hour of negro destiny in that island nearer and nearer, when Providence designed that he should play his part in the great drama of freedom that was then being enacted. Of course the propitious moment for the free men of color to begin to move would present itself prior to that for the movement of the negro slaves.

The opportunity for the men of color presented itself when the general colonial assembly of St. Marc's (already referred to) sent deputies to France, to present the result of its deliberations to the National Assembly; and to ask that august body to confer on the colony the right of self-government.

At this time, therefore, when the affairs of the colony were about to undergo examination in the supreme legislature of the mother country, the free men of color seized upon the occasion to send deputies to France also, men of their own caste, to represent their grievances and make their wishes known to the National Assembly. This discreet discernment of such an opportune moment to make such a movement divested of every other consideration, shows a people who understand themselves, what they want, and how to seek it.

But when we proceed to consider the most approved manner in which the representations were made to the National Assembly, by the colored delegates in behalf of their caste, in the colony of St. Domingo, and the influences they brought to bear upon that body, as exhibited hereafter: we shall perceive thereby that they showed such an intimate acquaintance with the secret springs of governmental machinery, as demonstrated at once their capacity to govern themselves.

This deputation first drew up a statement in behalf

of their caste in the colony, of such a stirring nature as would be certain to command the national sympathy in their cause, when presented to the National Assembly. But previously to presenting it to that assembly, they took the wise precaution to wait upon the honorable president of that august body, in order to enlist and commit him in their favor, as the first stepping stone to secure the success of their object before the Supreme Legislature.

They prevailed in their mission to the President of the Assembly; and succeeded in obtaining this very emphatic assurance from him: "No part of the nation shall vainly reclaim their rights before the assembly of the representatives of the French people."

Having accomplished this important step, the colored deputies next began to operate through the Abolition Society of Paris, called *"Les Amis des Noirs,"* upon such of the members of the assembly as were affiliated with this society, and thus already indirectly pledged to favor such a project as theirs, asking simple justice for their race. They were again successful, and Charles De Lameth, one of the zealous patrons of that society, and an active member of the National Assembly, was engaged to argue their cause before the Supreme Legislature of the nation, although strange to say, he was himself a colonial slaveholder at that time.

And at the appointed moment in the National Assembly, this remarkable man felt prompted to utter these astounding words in behalf of this oppressed and disfranchised class of the colony: "I am one of the greatest proprietors of St. Domingo; yet I declare to you, that sooner than lose sight of principles so sacred to justice and humanity, I would prefer to lose all that I possess. I declare myself in favor of admitting the men of color to the rights of citizenship; and in favor of the freedom of the blacks."

Now let us for a moment stop and reflect on the

measures resorted to by the colored deputies of St. Domingo, in Paris, who, by their wise stratagems, had brought their cause step by step to such an eventful and auspicious crisis as this.

Could there have been surer measures concocted for the success of their plans, than thus committing the president of the assembly to their cause in the first place; and afterwards pressing a liberty-loving slaveholder into their service, to thunder their measures through the National Assembly, by such a bold declaration?

Who among the old fogies of Tammany Hall—that junta of scheming politicans who govern this country by pulling the wires of party, and thereby making every official of the nation, from the President of the United States down to the Commissioners for Street Sweeping in the City of New York, dance as so many puppets at their bidding—I repeat it—who among these all-powerful but venal politicians of old Tammany, could have surpassed these tactics of those much abused men of color, who thus swayed the secret springs of the National Assembly of France? And who, after this convincing proof to the contrary, shall dare to say that the negro race is not capable of self-government?

But to return to the thread of our narrative. When the secret springs had been thus secured in their behalf, they had nothing to fear from the popular heart of the nation, already keenly alive to the sentiments of Liberty, Equality, and Fraternity; because the simple justice of their demands would commend them to the people as soon as they were publicly made known in France.

In order to make the very best impression on the popular heart of the nation, their petition demanding simple justice to their caste was accompanied with a statement very carefully drawn up.

In this statement they showed that their caste in the colony of St. Domingo possessed one-third of the real estate, and one-fourth of the personal effects of the island. They also set forth the advantages of their position in the political and social affairs of St. Domingo, as a balance of power in the hand of the imperial government of France, against the high pretensions of the haughty planters on the one hand, and the seditious spirit of the poor whites on the other. And, as an additional consideration, by way of capping the climax, they offered in the name, and in behalf of the free men of color in the colony, six millions of francs as a loyal contribution to the wants and financial exigencies of the National Treasury, to be employed in liquidating the debt of their common country.

Thus, if neither their wire-working maneuvers, the justice of their cause, nor yet the conservative influence which their position gave them in the colony, had been enough to secure the end which they sought; then the tempting glitter of so much cash, could not be resisted, when its ponderous weight was also thrown in the scale of justice. They succeeded, as a matter of course, in accomplishing their purpose; and the National Assembly of France promulgated a decree on the 8th of March, 1790, securing equal political rights to the men of color.

The very success of this movement, and the means by which its success was effected, the opportune moment when it was commenced, and the immense odds that were against those that sought its accomplishment—all these things must hereafter be emblazoned on the historic page as an everlasting tribute to the genius of the negro race, and remain an ineffaceable evidence of their capacity for self-government; that may be triumphantly adduced and proudly pointed at in this and every succeeding generation of the world, until the latest syllable of recorded time.

THE CRISIS PRODUCED IN THE COLONY BY THIS DECREE

THE MEN OF COLOR ON THE SIDE OF LIBERTY, LAW, AND ORDER

It was when this decree was made known in the colony of St. Domingo, that the General Assembly of the colony, then sitting at St. Marc's, expressed the malignant sentiments of the white colonists, in a resolution that I have already quoted, viz: they resolved that they would "Rather die, than share equal political rights with a bastard race."

Vincent Oje, a man of color, and one of the delegates to Paris, in behalf of his caste, anticipated a venomous feeling of this kind against his race, on the part of the white colonists, when these decrees should be made known to them. He however, resolved to do whatever was within his power, to allay this rancorous feeling. He did not therefore hasten home to the colony immediately after the decree was promulgated. He delayed, in order to allow time for their momentary excitement as expressed in the resolution above, to cool off, by a more calm reflection on their sober second thought. He also tarried in France, to secure a higher political end, by which he would be personally prepared to return to St. Domingo, to make the most favorable impression in behalf of his race, and the objects of that decree, on the minds of the white colonists.

To this end he succeeds in getting the appointment of Commissioner of France, from the French government, to superintend the execution of the decree of the 8th of March, 1790, in the island of St. Domingo.

Certainly, he might hope, that being invested with the sacred dignity of France, his person, his race, (thus honored through him by that imperial government,) and the National decree itself, with which he was charged, would now be respected.

But not content with accumulating the national honors of France; fearing lest the pro-Slavery colonists would disregard these high prerogatives, by looking upon them as having been obtained through the *fanatical* "Friends of the Blacks" at Paris, by those partisans exerting an undue influence on the National Government: he further proceeds to gather additional honors, by ingratiating himself into the favor of a potentate of Holland—the Prince of Limbourg; from whom he received the rank of Lieutenant Colonel, and the order of the Lion. Thus he wished to demonstrate to the infatuated colonists, who regarded his race as beneath their consideration, that he could not only obtain titles and reputation in France, by means of ardent friends, but that over and above these, and beyond the boundaries of France, he could also command an European celebrity.

This was indeed a splendid course of conduct on his part; and by thus gathering around him and centering within himself these commanding prestiges of respect, he demonstrated his thorough knowledge of one of the most important secrets in the art of governing; and so far made another noble vindication of the capacity of the negro race for self-government.

But as we proceed to consider the manner that he afterwards undertook to prosecute his high National Commission in promulgating in St. Domingo, the decree of the 8th of March, 1790, we shall see additional evidence of the same master skill crowd upon us.

He had now delayed his return from Europe in order to allow time for the allaying of hasty excitement, and for the purpose of making the most favorable advent to the island.

He comes a commissioned envoy of the French nation, and an honored chevalier of Europe. Nevertheless, with that prudent foresight which anticipates all possible emergencies, he landed in St. Domingo in a cautious and unostentatious manner, so as not to provoke any forcible demonstration against him. Having landed, he gathered around him a suite of 200 men for his personal escort, which his station justified him in having as his cortege; and which might also serve the very convenient purpose of a body guard to defend him against any attempt at a cowardly assassination from any lawless or ruthless desperadoes of oppression in the colony.

At the head of this body of men, he at once proceeded to place himself in communication with the Colonial Assembly, then in session; to inform it officially of his commission and the national decree which he bore; and to require that assembly, as the legislative authority of the island, to enforce its observance, by enacting an ordinance in accordance with the same.

In this communication of Oje, being aware of their pro-slavery prejudices, he endeavored to conciliate them by a peace offering. That peace offering was the sanctioning of Negro Slavery; for he stated to the assembly that the decree did not refer to the blacks in servitude; neither did the men of color, said he, desire to acknowledge their equality.

This specific assurance on the part of Oje, although it does not speak much for his high sense of justice, when abstractly considered; yet it shows as much wisdom and tact in the science of government, as is evinced by the sapient or *sap* headed legislators of this country, who make similar compromises as a peace offering to the prejudice and injustice of the oligarchic despots of this nation.

Oje, however, failed to make the desired impression on the infatuated colonists, either by his National and European dignities, or by his peace offering of 500,000 of his blacker brethren. He fell beneath the malignant hate of the slaveholding colonists, after defending himself with his little band of followers, against the overwhelming odds of these sanguinary tigers, with a manly heroism, only equalled by the Spartans at the pass of

Thermopylae, and thus has cut for himself an enduring niche among the heroes in the temple of fame.

He was captured; and after a mock trial, illustrative of pro-slavery justice; something similar, for instance, to our Fugitive Slave Law trials in Boston, Philadelphia, and Cincinnati—(though more merciful in its penalty than these)—this mock court of St. Domingo condemned Vincent Oje and his brave lieutenant, Jean Chevanne, with their surviving compatroits, to be broken alive on the wheel.

We foreget the error of the head committed by this right hearted, noble, and generous man, towards his more unfortunate brethren, in order to weep over his ignoble and unworthy fate, received at the hands of those monsters of cruelty in St. Domingo.

I cannot better close this notice of Oje, than by repeating the concluding lines from a Poem dedicated to him, by that distinguished man of color, our own fellow countryman, Prof. George B. Vashon, of McGrawville College:

> "Sad was your fate, heroic band,
>   Yet mourn we not, for yours the stand
>   Which will secure to you a fame,
>   That never dieth, and a name
>   That will, in coming ages be
>   A signal word for Liberty.
>   Upon the Slave's o'erclouded sky,
>   Your gallant actions traced the bow,
>   Which whispered of deliverance nigh—
>   The need of one decisive blow.
>   Thy coming fame, Oje! is sure;
>   Thy name with that of L'Ouverture,
>   And the noble souls that stood
>   With both of you, in times of blood,
>   Will live to be the tyrant's fear—
>   Will live, the sinking soul to cheer!"

THE HOUR OF DESTINY FOR THE BLACKS

This untimely death of the great leader of the men of color, served only to develop how plentifully the race was supplied with sagacious characters, capable of performing daring deeds—it served to show how well the race was supplied with the material out of which great leaders are made, at any moment, and for any exigency.

Now came the hour for the patient, delving black slave to begin to move. He has manfully bided his time, whilst the white colonists were rampant in pursuit of high political prerogatives; and he has remained quiet, whilst his brother—the freed man of color, has carried his cause demanding equal political rights, triumphantly through the National Assembly of France.

But most intolerable of all, he has been perfectly still, whilst his more fortunate brethren have offered even to strike hands with the vile oppressor in keeping the iron yoke on his neck.

Nevertheless, he has lived to see both of these classes foiled by the over-ruling hand of Providence, from interpreting the words "Liberty, Equality, and Fraternity," to suit their own selfish and narrow notions. He finds these two parties now at open hostilities with one another. He sees, on one hand, the despicable colonists inviting foreign aid into the island, to resist the execution of the National decree and to prop up their unhallowed cause by the dread alternative of treason and rebellion. Whilst on the other hand, he beholds the men of color fighting on the side of the nation, law, and order, against the white colonists. Amid this general commotion his pulsations grow quick, and he feels that the hour of destiny is coming for *even* him to strike.

Yet he still possesses his soul in patience until the destined moment. At last he hears that France now vacillates in carrying out the tardy measure of justice that her National Legislature had enacted. The mother country, that had so nobly commenced the work of justice, by the national decree, enfranchising the free men of color, now begins to recede from the high position she had assumed, in order to favor the frenzied prejudice of the infatuated colonists. The negro slave had hoped that by this national act of justice to the free man of color, that a permanent step had been taken towards universal emancipation, and consequently his own eventual disenthralment. With this hope he was willing to continue quietly to wear his galling chains, rejoicing in the newly acquired boon of his more fortunate brethen, as the earnest and pledge of his own future deliverance, by a similar act of national justice. Thus the way seemed already paved for a peaceful termination of his servitude.

But, I repeat it again, the toiling black slave at last hears that the National Government of France vacillates in her judgment, quails before the storm of pro-slavery invectives, hurled by the insensate bigots of St. Domingo against the men of color, and finally, she recedes from her high position by the National Assembly repealing the decree of the 8th of March, 1790. Thus the slaves' dawning ray of hope and liberty is extinguished, and there is nothing ahead but the impenetrable gloom of eternal slavery.

This, then, is the ominous moment reserved for the chained bondman to strike; and he rises now from his slumber of degredation in the terrific power of brute force. Bouckman, (called by a Haytian historian the Spartacus of his race,) was raised up as the leader of the insurgents, who directed their fury in the desperate struggle for liberty and revenge, until the work of devastation and death was spread throughout the island to the most frightful extent. He continued to ride on the storm of revolution in its hurricane march, with a fury that became intensified as it progressed, until the colonists, by some fortuitous circumstances, were enabled to wreak their vengeance on this negro hero.

But when this first hero of the slaves was captured and executed by their oppressors, like Oje, the first hero of the free men of color; the capacity of the race to furnish leaders equal to any emergency, was again demonstrated.

A triumvirate of negro and mulatto chieftains now succeeded these two martyred heroes.

Jean François, Biassou, and Jeannot, now appeared upon the stage of action, and directed the arms of the exasperated insurgents against a faithless nation, the cruel colonists and their English allies, whose aid these colonists had invited, in their treasonable resistance to the National decree, which Oje came from France to promulgate in the name of the nation.

In order to contend against such overwhelming odds effectually, and for the purpose of obtaining the necessary supply of arms and ammunition, the insurgents went over, for a time, to the service of Spain. This government had always regarded the French as usurpers in the island; and the Spaniards were therefore glad of any prospect of expelling the French colonists entirely from St. Domingo. Hence they gladly accepted the proffered service of the blacks as a means to effect this end.

However, we have no reason to regard the Spanish government as being more favorably disposed towards the blacks than that of France. We may rather conclude that Spain was willing to use the blacks to subserve her end, and afterwards would doubtless have endeavored to reduce them to a state of slavery again.

Nevertheless the black slaves and free men of color went over the cause of Spain, and used her to subserve their purpose in driving France not only to re-enact her previous decree in relation to the men of color; but also to proclaim the immediate emancipation of the blacks, and to invest them with equal political rights. For this purpose, three National Commissioners of France were sent to the island, bearing these decrees of the Supreme Government.

When this glorious result was thus triumphantly effected, they left the service of Spain and returned to the cause of France again.

During the struggles that took place while the insurgents were in the cause of Spain, the three leaders who headed them when they united with the Spaniards, were shifted, by the fortunes of war, from their chieftainship, and replaced by Toussaint and Rigaud—one a black, and the other a mulatto, when they returned to the service of France.

These two leaders, at the head of their respective castes in the service of France, fighting on the side of liberty, law, and order, compelled the turbulent and treasonable colonists to respect these last national decrees; drove their English allies from the colony, and extinguished the Spanish dominion therein, and thus reduced the whole island to the subjection of France.

When we duly consider this shrewd movement of the blacks in thus pressing Spain in their service at that critical moment, when every thing depended upon the decision of the hour, by which they were enabled to accomplish such a glorious result, we have thereby presented another strong and convincing proof of the capacity of the negro to adopt suitable means to accomplish great ends; and it therefore demonstrates in the most powerful manner, his ability for self-government.

THE AUSPICIOUS DAWN OF NEGRO RULE

Toussaint, by his acute genius and daring prowess, made himself the most efficient instrument in accomplishing these important results, contemplated by the three French Commissioners, who brought the last decrees of the National Assembly of France, proclaiming liberty throughout the island to all the inhabitants thereof; and thus, like another Washington, proved himself the regenerator and savior of his country.

On this account, therefore, he was solemnly invested with the executive authority of the colony; and their labors having been thus brought to such a satisfactory and auspicious result, two of the Commissioners returned home to France.

No man was more competent to sway the civil destinies of these enfranchised bondmen than he who had preserved such an unbounded control over them as their military chieftain, and led them on to glorious deeds amid the fortunes of warfare recently waged in that island. And no one else could hold that responsible position of an official mediator between them and the government of France, with so great a surety and pledge of their continued freedom, as Toussaint L'Ouverture. And there was no other man, in fine, that these rightfully jealous freemen would have permitted to carry out such stringent measures in the island, so nearly verging to serfdom, which were so necessary at that time in order to restore industry, but one of their own caste whose unreserved devotion to the cause of their freedom, placed him beyond the suspicion of any treacherous design to re-enslave them.

Hence, by these eminent characteristics possessed by Toussaint in a super excellent degree, he was the very man for the hour; and the only one fitted for the governorship of the colony calculated to preserve the interests of all concerned.

The leading Commissioners of France, then in the island, duly recognized this fact, and did not dispute with him the claim to this responsible position. Thus had the genius of Toussaint developed itself to meet an emergency that no other man in the world was so peculiarly prepared to fulfill; and thereby he has added another inextinguishable proof of the capacity of the negro for self-government.

But if the combination of causes, which thus pointed him out as the only man that could undertake the fulfillment of the gubernatorial duties, are such manifest proofs of negro capacity; then the manner in which we shall see that he afterwards discharged the duties of that official station, goes still further to magnify the self-evident fact of negro capability.

The means that he adapted to heal the internecine dissensions that threatened civil turmoil; and the manner that he successfully counteracted the machinations of the ambitious General Hedouville, a French Commissioner that remained in the colony, who desired to overthrow Toussaint, showed that the negro chieftain was no tyro in the secret of government.

He also established commercial relations between that island and foreign nations; and he is said to be the first statesman of modern times, who promulgated the doctrine of free trade and reduced it to practice. He also desired to secure a constitutional government to St. Domingo, and for this purpose he assembled around him a select council of the most eminent men in the colony, who drew up a form of constitution under his supervision and approval, and which he transmitted, with a commendatory letter to Napoleon Bonaparte, then First Consul of France, in order to obtain the sanction of the imperial government.

But that great bad man did not even acknowledge its receipt to Toussaint; but in his mad ambition he silently meditated when he should safely dislodge the negro chief from his responsible position, as the necessary prelude to the re-enslavement of his sable brethren, whose freedom was secure against his nefarious designs, so long as Toussaint stood at the helm of affairs in the colony.

But decidedly the crowning act of Toussaint

L'Ouverture's statesmanship, was the enactment of the
Rural Code, by the operation of which, he was successful
in restoring industrial prosperity to the island, which
had been sadly ruined by the late events of sanguinary
warfare. He effectually solved the problem of immediate
emancipation and unimpaired industry, by having the
emancipated slaves produce thereafter, as much of the
usual staple productions of the country, as was produced
under the horrible regime of slavery; nevertheless, the
lash was entirely abolished, and a system of wages
adopted, instead of the uncompensated toil of the lacer-
ated and delving bondman.

In fact, the island reached the highest degree of
prosperity that it ever attained, under the negro governorship of Toussaint.

The rural code, by which so much was accomplished,
instead of being the horrible nightmare of despotism—
worse than slavery, that some of the pro-slavery calumina-
tors of negro freedom and rule would have us believe;
was, in fact, nothing more than a prudent government
regulation of labor—a regulation which made labor the
first necessity of a people in a state of freedom,—a regulation which struck a death blow at idleness, the parent
of poverty and all the vices—a regulation, in fine, which
might be adopted with advantage in every civilized
country in the world, and thereby extinguish two-thirds
of the pauperism, vagrancy, and crime, that curse these
nations of the earth; and thus lessen the need for poor-
houses, police officers, and prisons, that are now sustained at such an enormous expense, for the relief of the
poor and the correction of felons.

This Haytian Code compelled every vagabond or
loafer about the towns and cities, who had no visible
means of an honest livelihood, to find an employer and
work to do in the rural districts. And if no private employer could be found, then the government employed
such on its rural estates, until they had found a private

employer. The hours and days of labor were prescribed by this code, and the terms of agreement and compensation between employer and employed were also determined by its provisions. Thus, there could be no private imposition on the laborers; and, as a further security against such a spirit, the government maintained rural magistrates and a rural police, whose duty it was to see to the faithful execution of the law on both sides.

By the arrangement of this excellent and celebrated code, everybody in the commonwealth was sure of work and compensation for the same, either from private employers or from the government. Nobody need fear being starved for want of work to support themselves, as is often the case among the laborers of Europe, and is fast coming to pass in the densely populated communities of this country, where labor is left to take care of itself under the private exploitation of mercenary capitalists. Under this code nobody need fear being exploited by such unprincipled and usurious men, who willingly take advantage of the poor to pay them starvation prices for their labor; because, against such, the law of Toussaint secured to each laborer a living compensation.

By the operation of this code, towns and cities were cleared of all those idle persons who calculate to live by their wits, and who commit nine-tenths of all the crimes that afflict civilized society. All such were compelled to be engaged at active industrial labors, and thus rendered a help to themselves and a blessing to the community at large.

By this industrial regulation, every thing flourished in the island in an unprecedented degree; and the negro genius of Toussaint, by a bold and straight-forward provision for the regulation and protection of his emancipated brethren, effected that high degree of prosperity in Hayti, which all the wisdom of the British nation has not been able to accomplish in her emancipated West India colonies, in consequence of her miserable shuffling

47

in establishing Coolie and Chinese apprenticeship—that semi-system of slavery—in order to gratify the prejudices of her pro-slavery colonial planters; and because of the baneful influence of absentee landlordism, which seems to be an inseparable incident of the British system of property.

Thus did the negro government of St. Domingo, show more paternal solicitude for the well being of her free citizens, than they ever could have enjoyed under the capricious despotism of individual masters who might pretend to care for them; and thus did it more truly subserve the purposes of a government than any or all of the similar organizations of civilization, whose only care and object seem to be the protection of the feudal rights of property in the hands of the wealthy few; leaving the honest labor of the many unprotected, and the poor laborer left to starve, or to become a criminal, to be punished either by incarceration in the jails, prisons and dungeons provided for common felons; or executed on the gallows as the greatest of malefactors.

The genius of Toussaint by towering so far above the common ideas of this age in relation to the true purposes of government; and by carrying out his bold problem with such eminent success, has thereby emblazoned on the historic page of the world's statemanship a fame more enduring than Pitt, who laid the foundation of a perpetual fund to liquidate the national debt of England.

I say Toussaint has carved for himself a more enduring fame, because his scheme was more useful to mankind. The negro statesman devised a plan that comprehended in its scope the well being of the masses of humanity. But Pitt only laid a scheme whereby the few hereditary paupers pensioned on a whole nation, with the absurd right to govern it, might still continue to plunge their country deeper and deeper into debt, to subserve their own extravagant purposes; and then provide for the payment of the same out of the blood and sweat, and bones of the delving operatives and colliers of Great Britain. Thus, then, Toussaint by the evident superiority of his statesmanship, has left on the pages of the world's statute book, an enduring and irrefutable testimony of the capacity of the negro for self-government, and the loftiest achievements in national statesmanship.

And Toussaint showed that he had not mistaken his position by proving himself equal to that trying emergency when that demigod of the historian Abbott, Napoleon Bonaparte, first Consul of France, conceived the infernal design of reenslaving the heroic blacks of St. Domingo; and who for the execution of this nefarious purpose sent the flower of the French Army, and a naval fleet of fifty-six vessels under command of General Leclerc, the husband of Pauline, the voluptuous and abandoned sister of Napoleon.

When this formidable expedition arrived on the coast of St. Domingo, the Commander found Toussaint and his heroic compeers ready to defend their God given liberty against even the terrors of the godless First Consul of France. Wheresoever these minions of slavery and despotism made their sacrilegious advances, devastation and death reigned under the exasperated genius of Toussaint.

He made that bold resolution and unalterable determination, which, in ancient times, would have entitled him to be deified among the gods; that resolution was to reduce the fair eden-like Isle of Hispaniola to a desolate waste like Sahara; and suffer every black to be immolated in a manly defense of his liberty, rather than the infernal and accursed system of negro slavery should again be established on that soil. He considered it far better, that his sable countrymen should be DEAD FREEMEN than LIVING SLAVES.

The French veterans grew pale at the terrible man-

ner that the blacks set to work to execute this resolution.
Leclerc found it impossible to execute his design by
force; and he was only able to win the reconciliation of
the exasperated blacks to the government of France, by
abandoning his hostilities and pledging himself to respect their freedom thereafter. It was then that the brave
Negro Generals of Toussaint went over in the service of
Leclerc; and it was then, that the Negro Chieftain himself, resigned his post to the Governor General appointed
by Napoleon, and went into the shades of domestic re-
tirement, at his home in Ennery.

Thus did Toussaint, by his firm resolution to execute his purpose, by his devotion to liberty and the cause
of his race, so consistently maintained under all circumstances, more than deify himself; he proved himself more
than a patriot; he showed himself to be the unswerving
friend and servant of God and humanity.

Now, with the illustrious traits of character of this
brilliant negro before us, who will dare to say that the
race who can thus produce such a noble specimen of a
hero and statesman, is incapable of self-government? Let
such a vile slanderer, if there any longer remains such,
hide his diminutive head in the presence of his illustrious
negro superior!

I know it may be said that, after all Toussaint was
found wanting in the necessary qualities to meet, and
triumph in, the last emergency, when he was finally be-
guiled, and sent to perish in the dungeons of France, a
victim of the perfidious machinations of the heartless
Napoleon.

On this point I will frankly own that Toussaint was
deficient in those qualities by which his antagonist finally
succeeded in getting him in his power.

So long as manly skill and shrewdness—so long as
bold and open tactics and honorable strateagems were resorted to, the black had proved himself, in every respect,
the equal of the white man. But the negro's heart had

not yet descended to that infamous depth of subtle depravity, that could justify him in solemnly and publicly taking an oath, with the concealed, jesuitical purpose, of thereby gaining an opportunity to deliberately violate the same. He had no conception, therefore, that the white man from whom he had learned all that he knew of true—religion, I repeat it—he had no conception that the white man, bad as he was, slaveholder as he was—that *even* HE was really so debased, vile, and depraved, as to be capable of such a double-dyed act of villainy, as breaking an oath solemnly sealed by invoking the name of the Eternal God of Ages.

Hence, when the Captain General, Leclerc, said to Toussaint, in presence of the French and Black Generals, uplifting his hand and jewelled sword to heaven: "I swear before the face of the Supreme Being, to respect the liberty of the people of St. Domingo," Toussaint believed in the sincerity of this solemn oath of the white man. He threw down his arms, and went to end the remainder of his days in the bosom of his family. This was, indeed, a sad mistake for him, to place so much confidence in the word of the white man. As the result of this first error, he easily fell into another equally treacherous. He was invited by General Brunet, another minion of Napoleon, in St. Domingo, to partake of the social hospitalities of his home; but, Toussaint, instead of finding the domestic civilities that he expected, was bound in chains, sent on board the Hero, a vessel already held in readiness for the consummation of the vile deed, in which he was carried a prisoner to France.

That magnanimous man bitterly repented at his leisure, his too great confidence in the word of the white man, in the cold dark dungeons of the castle of Joux. And the depth of this repentance was intensified by a compulsory fast ordered by that would-be great and magnanimous man, Napoleon Bonaparte, who denied him food, and starved him to death.

Great God! how the blood runs chill, in contemplating the ignoble end of the illustrious negro chieftain and statesman, by such base and perfidious means!

A BLOODY INTERLUDE FINALLY ESTABLISHES NEGRO SOVEREIGNTY

But if the godlike Toussaint had thus proved himself deficient in those mean and unhallowed qualities that proved his sad overthrow, nevertheless, the race again proved itself equal to the emergency, by producing other leaders to fill up the gap now left open.

The negro generals, who had gone over to the service of France, on the solemn assurances and protestations of Leclerc, soon learned to imitate this new lesson of treachery, and accordingly deserted his cause, and took up arms against France again.

And, if afterwards, the heroic but sanguinary black chief, Dessalines, who had previously massacred 500 innocent whites (if any of these treacherous colonists can be called innocent) at Mirebalais; 700 more at Verettes, and several hundred others at La Riviere—I say again, if we now see him resume his work of slaughter and death, and hang 500 French prisoners on gibbets erected in sight of the very camp of General Rochambeau, we may see in this the bitter fruit of the treachery of the whites, in this dreadful reaction of the blacks.* These were the roots springing up, which Toussaint spoke of so sorrowfully on the ship's deck, as he was borne away a prisoner to France, from the coast of St. Domingo. The captive hero, on this occasion, compared himself to a tree, saying: "They have cut down in me the trunk of the tree; but the roots are many and deep." The furious Dessalines was, therefore, one of the foremost and firmest of these roots left in

---

* General Leclerc had now fallen a victim to the ravages of yellow fever, and Rochambeau had succeeded to the supreme command of the invading forces.

St. Domingo by the fallen chief, Toussaint, who soon sprung up into a verdant and luxurious growth of sanguinary deeds, by which the independence of his Island home was baptized in a Sea of Blood.

Finally, if we see Dessalines with red hot shot, prepared to sink the squadron of general Rochambeau, as it departed [for] France, although the negro chief had solemnly stipulated to allow it to sail from the harbor unmolested, we find in this determination of the bloodthirsty man, how well he had learned the lesson of treachery and perfidy from the example of the white man.

Thus, if shocking depravity in perfidiousness and covenant breaking, is needed as another evidence of the negro's equality with the white man, in order to prove his ability to govern himself, then the implacable black chief, Dessalines, furnishes us with that proof.

I think, however, we may thank God, that the last act of destruction contemplated by Dessalines was not consummated, in consequence of an English fleet taking Rochambeau and his squadron as prisoners of war in the harbor of Port-au-Prince; and thus, by this providential interposition, saved the race from a stigma on the pages of history, as foul as that which darkens the moral character of their antagonists.

Having now arrived at the epoch when the banners of negro independence waved triumphantly over the Queen of the Antilles; if we look back at the trials and tribulations through which they came up to this point of National regeneration, we have presented to us, in the hardy endurance and perseverance manifested by them, in the steady pursuit of Liberty and Independence, the overwhelming evidence of their ability to govern themselves. For fourteen long and soul-trying years— twice the period of the revolutionary struggle of this country—they battled manfully for freedom. It was on the 8th of March, 1790, as we have seen, that the immortal man of color, Vincent Oje, obtained a decree from the

National Assembly guaranteeing equal political privileges to the free men of color in the island. And, after a continued sanguinary struggle dating from that time, the never-to-be-forgotten self-emancipated black slave, Jean Jacques Dessalines, on the 1st of January, 1804, proclaimed negro freedom and independence throughout the island of St. Domingo.

That freedom and independence are written in the world's history in the ineffaceable characters of blood; and its crimsoned letters will ever testify of the determination and of the ability of the negro to be free, throughout the everlasting succession of ages.

EVIDENCES OF SELF-GOVERNMENT SINCE 1804

I will now proceed to give a hasty synopsis of the evidences that the Haytians have continued to manifest since their independence in demonstration of the Negroes' ability to govern themselves.

Dessalines the Liberator of his country was chosen as a matter of course the first Ruler of Hayti. During his administration, the efficient organization of an army of 60,000 men to defend the country against invaders—the erection of immense fortifications, and the effort to unite and consolidate the Spanish part of the Island in one government with the French portion over which he presided, showed that he understood the precautionary measures necessary to preserve the freedom and independence of his country; and so far he kept up the character of the race for capacity in self-government.

In the succeeding administrations of the rival chiefs, Christophe and Petion, we have indeed the sorrowful evidence of division, between the blacks and the men of color or mulattoes, the seeds of which were planted in the days of slavery. Nevertheless in that mutual good understanding that existed between them by which it was agreed to unite together whenever a foreign foe invaded the island; and in the contemptuous manner that both chiefs rejected the perfidious overtures of Bonaparte, we have still the evidence of that conservative good sense which fully exhibits the negroes ability to take care of himself.

In the next administration of Boyer where we find these divisions in the French part of the island happily healed; and the Spanish colony also united in one government with the French, as Dessalines ardently desired in his time; we have the most astonishing evidence of the perfection the black race could make in the art of self-government, during the short period of twenty years independence.

After Boyer's administration there were some slight manifestations of disorder, arising from the smouldering feud between the blacks and men of color that the ancient regime of slavery had created among them; the baneful influence of which the work of freedom and independence has not yet had time to entirely efface. In this disorder we find the Spanish part of the island secede and set up a separate nationality.—But we find every thing in the French part soon settling down into order again, under the vigorous sceptre of the present ruler, Faustin I.

And in his known sentiments to harmonize all classes of his people, and to unite the whole island under one strong government, to secure which end he has exerted every influence within his power, we have the continued evidence of those large and extended views of national policy among the rules of Hayti, that proves their ability to govern themselves in a manner that will compare favorably with the statesmanship of any existing government of modern civilization.

Here we shall rest the evidence in proof of the competency of the negro race for self-government which we have drawn out to rather a protracted length for the space assigned to a single Lecture; and turn our attention now to some of the evidences of civilized progress evinced by that people. We shall be brief in the elucidation of this point, because as their ample competency to govern themselves, has now been firmly established from the highest point of view, this fact of itself demonstrates that the soundest elements of civilized progress are inherent among such a people. Nevertheless it will be well to particularize some of the proofs on this point also.

EVIDENCES OF CIVILIZED PROGRESS

NATIONAL ENTERPRISE

Under the administration of Dessalines aside from the military preparations we have noticed; he continued the Code Rural of Toussaint as the law of the land, thereby demonstrating that the negro in independence could carry forward measures of industry for his own benefit as well as for the whites when he governed for and in the name of France; for such was the case during the Governor Generalship of Toussaint. He also established schools in nearly every district of his dominions, and the people seeing what advantage was possessed by those who had received instruction, attached great importance to its acquisition; and as the result in a short time there were but few who did not learn to read and white.

In the constitution that he promulgated, it was declared that he who was not a good father, a good husband, and above all a good soldier, was unworthy to be called a Haytian citizen. It was not permitted fathers to disinherit their children; and every person was required by law to exercise some mechanical art or handicraft.

Thus fundamental measures were taken to make education, well regulated families and the mechanic arts, those three pillars of civilization, the basis of Haytian Society.—And in this fact where such high necessities were recognized and appreciated, we have the most undoubted evidence of civilized progress.

The overthrow of the government of Dessalines, by the spontaneous uprising of the people in their majesty, when it had become a merciless and tyrannical despotism, may also be noted here as another evidence of progress in political freedom of thought that made the race scorn to be tyrannized over by an oppressive master, whether that master was a cruel white tyrant, or a merciless negro despot.

Passing on to the two-fold government of Petion and Christophe, we not only discover the same military vigilance kept up by the construction of the tremendous fortification called the Citadel Henry that was erected by Christophe, under the direction of European Engineers, mounting 300 cannons;—but we also find both of these chiefs introducing teachers from Europe in their respective dominions; and establishing the Lancasterian system of schools.

We discover also during their administration, Protestant Missionaries availing themselves of the tolerant provision in regard to religious worship that had been maintained in the fundamental laws of the country since the days of Dessalines. These Missionaries commenced their work of evangelization with the approbation of the negro and mulatto chieftains;—and Christophe went so far as to import a cargo of Bibles for gratuitous distribution among his people.

Thus do we find that progress continued to make its steady steps of advancement among these people, notwithstanding the political divisions that had now taken place among them.

The succeeding administration of General Jean Pierre Boyer, under whom these divisions were happily healed, was fraught with stupendous projects of advancement.

The whole of the laws of the island were codified and made simple, under six different heads, viz: The Code Rural, the Civil Code, the Commercial Code, the Criminal Code, and the Code of Civil and Criminal procedure, regulating the practice in the several courts of the island. Thus, by this codification of her laws, did Hayti execute over thirty years ago, that which the States of this Union are just arousing to the necessity of doing. Boyer also set on foot a project of emigration, for the purpose of inducing the colored people of the United States to remove to Hayti, in order to replenish and accelerate the growth of the Haytian population. This project resulted in the removal of 6,000 colored people to that island from this country.

In addition to this important movement, various enterprises were undertaken by men of public spirit, during this administration, to promote industry among the people of Hayti.

A company was formed to carry on a mahogany saw mill, which expended $20,000 in the purchase of the necessary machinery from France. The mill was erected at St. Marc's. Judge Lespinasse, chief justice of the Court of Cassation, was President of the Company; and it was under the special patronage of General Boyer, the President of the Republic.

Another company was also formed, under the presidency of Senator Jorge, for tanning purposes, and expended $10,000 in preparations for carrying on the business. A saw mill was also erected at Port-au-Prince, by a private individual, at the cost of $15,000.

Thus were the most vigorous efforts of progress manifested during the administration of Boyer.

In the subsequent administration of Guerrier, Pierrot, and Riviere, which followed each other in quick and rather chaotic succession, the work of industrial progress did not abate. Two steamers were purchased by the government, a model agricultural farm was established under a scientific director from France; and English architects, carpenters, and stone masons were hired to come in the country to improve the style of building.

Finally, we also discover the same evidences of gradual progress, when we come down to the present administration of Faustin I. A navy of about twenty armed vessels has been created. Thirteen steam sugar mills have been erected. The system of education improved and extended. And a house of industry erected at Port-au-Prince, for the purpose of instructing boys in the mechanic arts.

And here let me add, that during the whole period of these successive administrations, that we have thus summarily passed under review, a thrifty commercial trade has been maintained between that island and the maritime nations of Europe and America, amounting in the aggregate, to several millions of dollars per annum.

Hence, these evidences of educational and industrial development, expanding continually as years roll onward, we regard as the most irrefragable proof of true civilized progress on the part of the Haytian people.

STABILITY OF THE GOVERNMENT

But in addition to these facts, we may adduce the general stability of the government they have maintained, as another evidence of civilized progress. There have been but eight rulers in Hayti since 1804, counting separately, Christophe and Petion, who ruled cotemporaneously. This is a period of fifty-three years down to the present time. And in the United States, since 1809, there have been ten different chief magistrates—a period of forty-eight years. Thus, this country has had two more rulers than Hayti, within a period five years less than the Haytian sovereignty.

The fact is, there is no nation in North America, but the United States, nor any in South America, except

Brazil, that can pretend to compare with Hayti, in respect to general stability of government. The Spanish Republics of America will have as many different rules in eight years as Hayti has had in a half century. And the colonial dependencies of European nations change governors at least three times as often as that negro nation has done. This political stability, therefore, on the part of the Haytians, indicates a vast remove from Barbarism. It is far ahead of the anarchy of some so-called civilized nations. And it therefore indicates a high degree of civilization and progress.

Some exceptions might be taken, by the over scrupulous partizan of popular institutions, at the tendency manifested to vacillate between a Republican and Monarchial form of government, that has constantly been exhibited in Hayti, since the days of Dessalines.

The desire for Republican institutions has its rise in the Cosmopolitan ideas and example of France, at the time of the Haytian Revolution. The proximate example of the United States may also influence this desire for republicanism to some extent.

On the other hand, Monarchy is an ancient traditionary predilection of the race derived from Africa, which ancient continent maintains that form of government in common with the rest of the old world. The gorgeous splendor and august prestige of aristrocratic rank and title, always attendant on this form of government, hold an imperious sway over the minds of this race of men who have such a keen appreciation of the beautiful. With these monarchical instincts on the one hand, and those powerful republican influencies on the other, Hayti has continually oscillated between a republican and a monarchical form of government. But be it ever remembered to her credit, this oscillation has not unsettled the permanent stability of her national administration, as the facts previously adduced, abundantly prove.

Permit me, however to urge with due deference to the republican ideas which surround me, that it matters not in the eternal principles of morality, what the form of government may be, so long as the ruling powers of a nation maintain the inviolability of personal liberty, exact justice and political equality among all of its honest citizens and subjects. If these things are not so maintained, a republic is as great, nay a greater despotism than an autocracy.

If there is but one despot to oppress the people, then there is but one neck to be severed in order to rid the earth of such a loathesome pest. But if the petty despots are numbered by the millions; then woe to that proscribed class that may fall under their tyranny, for it will need more axes and more executioners than can be supplied, in order to get this countless brood out of the way.

A popular despotism therefore, whose rulers are composed of political gamblers for the spoils of office and burglarious plunderers of the public treasury that tyran[n]izes over any class of its citizens and subject[s], is less tolerable than a monarchical or an aristocratic despotism, even though its rulers are a hereditary class of blood-titled paupers pensioned from generation to generation, on the public bounty of the nation. Among this latter class of rulers there is not to be found such a desperate and reckless set of lawless adventurers as will be found among the former. And should such monsters present themselves, they are in a more tangible shape to be got at and disposed of in a government of the few, than in that of the many. Hence the sacred purposes of government in securing the welfare of the whole people will always be more nearly arrived at in the one than in the other.

The Haytian people when governed by the crowned and imperial Dessalines testified their love of liberty, by destroying the tyrant when he violated the constitution and overstepped the laws of his country.

The American people under a republican form of government manifest their want of a love of true liberty, when they permit a vagabond set of politicians, whose character for rowdyism disgraces the nation, to enact such an odious law as the Fugitive Slave bill, violating the writ of *Habeas Corpus,* and other sacred guarantees of the Constitution;—and then tamely submit to this high handed outrage, because such unprincipled scoundrels voted in their insane revelry, that it must be the Supreme law of the land.

If there was one-half of the real love of liberty among even the people of the professedly free northern states, as there is among the negroes of Hayti, every one of their national representatives who voted for that infamous bill, or who would not vote instantaneously for its repeal, would be tried for his life, condemned and publicly executed as accessory to man stealing. Thus would a free people, determined to preserve their liberties, rid themselves of a brood of petty tyrants who seek to impose their unhallowed partizan caprices upon the country, as the supreme law of the land, over-riding even the Higher Law of God. And thus in time would they exhibit an equally jealous regard for their rights, as the Haytians did, when they rid themselves of the tyrant Dessalines.

If such was the real love of liberty among the northern people of this vain-glorious Republic, we should soon annihilate that morally spineless class of politicians, who need decision of character, when they get to Washington, to legislate for freedom. All such as were thus morally destitute of spinal vertebrae to resist the aggressions of the slave power, in the National Halls of legislation, would also soon be physically deficient in their cervical vertebrae, when they returned home, to meet the extreme penalty of an outraged and indignant constituency.

But such a determined spirit of liberty does not exist here, and honest men must submit therefore with lamb-like patience to this republican despotism of irresponsible political partizans who violate every just principle of law, because these unrighteous decrees are perpetrated in the name of the sovereign people.

Hence there is far more security for personal liberty and the general welfare of the governed, among the monarchical negroes of Hayti where the rulers are held individually responsible for their public acts, than exists in this bastard democracy.

The single necked despot is soon reached by the keen avenging axe of liberty, for any acts of despotism among the Haytian blacks; but here its dull and blunted edge lies useless; for it might be hurled in vain and fall powerless among a nameless crowd of millions.

CONCLUSION

But our historical investigations are at an end, and we must hasten to bring our reflections to a conclusion. I have now fulfilled my design in vindicating the capacity of the negro race for self-government and civilized progress against the unjust aspersions of our unprincipled oppressors, by boldly examining the facts of Haytian history and deducing legitimate conclusions therefrom. I have summoned the sable heroes and statesmen of that independent isle of the Caribbean Sea, and tried them by the high standard of modern civilization, fearlessly comparing them with the most illustrious men of the most enlightened nations of the earth;—and in this examination and comparison the negro race has not fallen one whit behind their contemporaries. And in this investigation I have made no allowance for the negroes just emerging from a barbarous condition and out of the brutish ignorance of West Indian slavery. I have been careful not to make such an allowance, for fear that instead of proving negro equality only, I should prove negro superiority. I shun the point of making this allowance to the negro, as it might reverse the case of the question entirely, that I have been combatting and instead of disproving his alleged inferiority only, would on the other hand, go farther, and establish his superiority. Therefore as it is my design to banish the words "superiority" and "inferiority" from the vocabulary of the world, when applied to the natural capacity of races of men, I claim no allowance for them on the score of their condition and circumstances.

Having now presented the preceding array of facts and arguments to establish, before the world, the negro's equality with the white man in carrying forward the great principles of self-government and civilized progress; I would now have these facts exert their legitimate influence over the minds of my race, in this country, in producing that most desirable object of arousing them to a full consciousness of their own inherent dignity; and thereby increasing among them that self-respect which shall urge them on to the performance of those great deeds which the age and the race now demand at their hands.

Our brethren of Hayti, who stand in the vanguard of the race, have already made a name, and a fame for us, that is as imperishable as the world's history. They exercise sovereign authority over an island, that in natural advantages, is the Eden of America, and the garden spot of the world. Her rich resources invite the capacity of 10,000,000 human beings to adequately use them. It becomes then an important question for the negro race in America to well consider the weighty responsibility that the present exigency devolves upon them, to contribute to the continued advancement of this negro nationality of the New World until its glory and renown shall overspread and cover the whole earth, and redeem and regenerate by its influence in the future, the benighted Fatherland of the race in Africa.

Here in this black nationality of the New World,

erected under such glorious auspices, is the stand point
that must be occupied, and the lever that must be exerted, to regenerate and disenthrall the oppression and
ignorance of the race, throughout the world. We must not
overlook this practical vantage ground which Providence
has raised up for us out of the depths of the sea, for any
man-made and utopian scheme that is prematurely forced
upon us, to send us across the ocean, to rummage the
graves of our ancestors, in fruitless, and ill-directed efforts
at the wrong end of human progress. Civilization and
Christianity is passing from the East to the West; and its
pristine splendor will only be rekindled in the ancient
nations of the Old World, after it has belted the globe in
its westward course, and revisted the Orient again. The
serpentine trail of civilization and Christianity, like the
ancient philosophic symbol of eternity, must coil backward to its fountain head. God, therefore in permitting
the accursed slave traffic to transplant so many millions
of the race, to the New World, and educing therefrom
such a negro nationality as Hayti, indicates thereby, that
we have a work now to do here in the Western World,
which in his own good time shall shed its orient beams
upon the Fatherland of the race. Let us see to it, that
we meet the exigency now imposed upon us, as nobly on
our part at this time as the Haytians met theirs at the
opening of the present century. And in seeking to perform this duty, it may well be a question with us, whether
it is not our duty, to go and identify our destiny with
our heroic brethren in that independent isle of the
Caribbean Sea, carrying with us such of the arts, sciences
and genius of modern civilization, as we may gain from
this hardy and enterprising Anglo-American race, in order to add to Haytian advancement; rather than to indo-
lently remain here, asking for political rights, which, if
granted, a social proscription stronger than conventional
legislation will ever render nugatory and of no avail
for the manly elevation and general well-being of the

race. If one powerful and civilized negro sovereignty can be developed to the summit of national grandeur in the West Indies, where the keys to the commerce of both hemispheres can be held; this fact will solve all questions respecting the negro, whether they be those of slavery, prejudice or proscription, and wheresoever on the face of the globe such questions shall present themselves for a satisfactory solution.

A concentration and combination of the negro race, of the Western Hemisphere in Hayti, can produce just such a national development. The duty to do so, is therefore incumbent on them. And the responsibility of leading off in this gigantic enterprise Providence seems to have made our peculiar task by the eligibility of our situation in this country, as a point for gaining an easy access to that island. Then let us boldly enlist in this high pathway of duty, while the watchwords that shall cheer and inspire us in our noble and glorious undertaking, shall be the soul-stirring anthem of GOD and HUMANITY.

A SUMMER

ON

THE BORDERS

OF

THE CARIBBEAN SEA

BY J. DENNIS HARRIS

ADVERTISEMENT

T H R O U G H the columns of leading journals in New York, St. Louis, and other localities, we have had occasion to acknowledge the fact that the political views which gave rise to the present volume, though comparatively new, have generally met the approval of distinguished statesmen and philanthropists, North and South.*

The following note from the venerable Mr. Giddings indicating the proposition, is but one of a large number which we have received from various parts of the country:—

Jefferson, Ohio, July 13, 1859

M y D e a r S i r :—I am heartily in favor of Mr. Blair's plan of furnishing territory in Central America for the use of such of our African brethren as wish to settle in a climate more congenial to the colored race than any that our government possesses.

I hope and trust you may be successful in your efforts.

Very truly,

J . D . H a r r i s , E s q .   J. R. GIDDINGS

The subjoined, respecting the work itself, is from Mr. William Culler Bryant, by whom, in addition to Mr. George W. Curtis, a portion of these communications was reviewed:—

Roslyn, Long Island, August 26, 1860

D e a r S i r :—I have looked over with attention the letters you left with me, and return them herewith. It appears to me it will be very well to publish them. Of the Spanish part of the island of San Domingo very little is known—much less than of the French part; and the information you give of the country and its people is valuable and interesting.

I am, Sir,

Respectfully yours,

M r . J . D . H a r r i s   W. C. BRYANT

---

* See Appendix.

Contents

DOMINICAN REPUBLIC

REPUBLIC OF HAYTI

HISTORICAL SKETCH

Introduction

The free colored American, of whatever shade, sees that his destiny is linked with slavery. Where his face is a crime he can not hope for justice. In the country which enslaves his race he can never be an acknowledged man. That it is his native country does not help him. The author of this book is an American as much as James Buchanan. He is more so: for the father of Mr. Buchanan was born in Ireland, and the father of Mr. Harris was born in North Carolina. But the one becomes president; the other is officially declared to have no rights which white men are bound to respect.

The intelligent colored man, therefore, as he ponders the unhappy condition of his race among us, perceives that, even if slavery in the Southern States were to be immediately abolished, his condition would be only nominally and legally, not actually, equal to that of the whites. The traditional habit of unquestioned mastery can not be laid aside at will. Prejudice is not amenable to law. There is a terrible logic in the slave system. For the proper and safe subjugation of the slave there must be silence, ignorance, and absolute despotism. But these react upon the master; and the difficulties and dangers of emancipation, as the history of Jamaica shows, are found upon the side of the master and not of the slave. The law might establish a political equality between them, but the old feeling would survive, and would still exclaim with the San Domingo planters when the French Assembly freed the mulattoes in 1791, "We would rather die than share our political rights with a bastard and degenerate race."

The free colored man, wishing to help himself and his race, may choose one of several methods. If he dare to take the risk, he may try to recover by force the rights of which force only deprives him. But his truest friends among the dominant race will assure him that such a course is mere suicide. In a war of races in this country his own would be exterminated. Or he may say with Geo. T. Downing, "I feel that I am working for the people with whom I am identified in oppression, in securing a business name: I shall strive for my and their elevation, but it will be by a strict and undivided attention to business." Or he may believe with Jefferson, "Nothing is more certainly written in the book of fate than that these people [the colored] are to be free: nor is it less certain that the two races equally free can not live in the same government. Nature, habit, opinion, have drawn indissoluble lines of distinction between them."

This latter opinion is shared by many intelligent public men in this country, of whom Francis P. Blair, Jr., of Missouri, Senator Doolittle, of Wisconsin, and Senator Bingham, of Michigan, are the most conspicuous. They believe that the emigration of free colored people, protected by the United States, into some region of propitious climate and beyond the taint of prejudice against color, would have the most important practical influence upon the question of emancipation in this country, and of the consequent restoration of the colored race to the respect of the world.

It is not surprising that a docile and amiable people enslaved by nearly half the States,—legally excluded from many of the rest, and everywhere contemned, should believe this, and turn their eyes elsewhere in the fond faith that any land but their own is friendly.

The author of this book is of opinion that under the protection of the United States government a few intelligent and industrious colored families could colonize some spot within the Gulf of Mexico or upon its shores, and there live usefully and respected; while gradually an accurate knowledge of the advantages of such a settlement would be spread among their friends in the United States, and, as they developed their capacities for labor and society, not only attract their free brethren to follow, but enable the well-disposed slaveholders to see an easy and simple solution of the question which so deeply perplexes them, "What should we do with the emancipated slaves?"

But neither Mr. Harris nor his friends, so far as I know, anticipate the final solution of the practical problem of slavery by emigration. They do not contemplate any vast exodus of their race; for they know how slowly even the small results they look for must be achieved, since the first condition is the protection of the American government. Mr. Harris thinks that the island of Hayti or San Domingo, in its eastern or Dominican portion, offers the most promising prospect for such an experiment; and this little book is the record of his own travel and observation upon that island and at other points of the Caribbean sea. It contains a brief and interesting sketch of the insurrection of Toussaint L'Ouverture, a story which incessantly reminds every thoughtful man that slavery everywhere, however seemingly secure, is only a suppressed, not an extinguished, volcano.

I commend the book heartily as sincere and faithful, quite sure that it will command attention not only by its intrinsic interest and merit, but as another silent and eloquent protest against the system which, while it deprives men of human rights, also denies them intellectual capacity. I think we may pardon the author that he does not love the government of his native land. But surely he and all other colored men may congratulate themselves that the party whose principles will presently control that government repeats the words of the Declaration of Independence as its creed of political philosophy.

GEORGE WILLIAM CURTIS

NEW YORK, *September 1st,* 1860.

75

A SUMMER ON THE BORDERS OF THE CARIBBEAN SEA

LETTER I

Dominican Republic

From New York to Puerto Del Plata — Smoothness of the Voyage — Hayti in the Distance — Description of the Standing Army — Unparalleled Scenic Beauty.

> "Is John departed, and is Lilburn gone?
> Farewell to both, to Lilburn and to John."
>   HUDIBRAS

It was a mild, showery morning on the 19th of May, 1860, that the brig John Butler, on board of which we were, left her dock at New York and anchored off the Jersey Flats. From this point we enjoyed the pleasantest and decidedly most satisfactory view of the great commercial city and its environs. The many white-sailed vessels and finely-painted steamers plying in and out the North and East rivers, and between the bright green undulating slopes of Staten and Long islands, presented a picturesque and animated scene, quite in contrast with the dark walls and stately steeples of the city which arose beyond.

More delightfully refreshing nothing could have been. Altogether, the fine air and characteristic scenes of New York bay amply repaid the inconvenience of remaining all day in sight of the great metropolis, without being jostled in its streets or snuffing the peculiar atmosphere that pervades it.

On the morning of the 20th we sailed out of the bay, passed Sandy Hook, and were at sea. The sky was

77

clear, and the ocean calm. Betwixt the novelty of being at sea for the first time and the dread of that sickness which all landsmen fear, but know to be inevitable, I was kept in a state of moderate excitement which effectually annihilated those sentimental sorrows which one is expected at such times to entertain. The first vessel we met coming in was the Porto Plata, from this city, and owned by a German firm on the corner of Broadway and Wall street, New York. Her cargo, I have since learned, consisted principally of mahogany and hides.

Our mornings were passed mostly in studying the Dominican language, which, as nearly as I can analyze it, is a compound of Spanish, French, English, Congo, and Caribbean—but, of course, principally Spanish. The afternoons were spent in fishing, and catching sea-weed, watching the flying-fish, or in looking simply and silently on the ever-bounding sea, which was in itself an infinite and unwearying source of irrepressible delight. A comparatively quiet sameness characterized the voyage. With bright clouds pencilling the sunset sky, a fresh breeze stiffening the sails, and the ship gliding smoothly over the buoyant waves, the sensations were at time exceedingly exhilarating, and even supremely delicious. But there were no dead calms, no terrific storms. To-day was the pale blue sky above, and the deep blue ocean rolling everywhere around; and to-morrow the sky was equally as fine, and the same dark heaving ocean as boundlessly sublime. Would there had been a storm, if only for description's sake!

But the poetry ceased. We were now in the latitude of the regular trade-winds, with which every man is supposed to be as certainly familiar as he is with a schoolbook, or the way to church. Where were the winds? Wanting—from the south and east when they should have been from the west, and *vice versa*. As for their reputed regularity, they were no more regular than a sinner at prayers. Four successive days we averaged about one mile an hour, and this was in the trade-winds! For the honor of all concerned, however, I will say (on the point-blank oath of our captain) that such a thing never occurred before, and, as he expressed it, "mightn't be again in a thousand years." I thought of an old man who once went travelling, and when he returned he was asked what he had learned. He said, simply, "I was a fool before, but by travelling I found it out." The astounding thunderstorms you hear about in the West Indies were all gone before we got here; so were the whirlwinds.

After a sail of twelve days, a long, dim, bluish outline, as of a cloud four hundred miles in length, stood out above the waves. Soon, with a glass, could be distinguished the regularly rising tablelands and lovely green valleys, the dark mountains standing in the background. I was at once agitated with all the anxieties of hope and fear. We were approaching the eventful shores of San Domingo, embracing as it does Dominican and Haytien republics. But however thrillingly interesting its past history may have been, the *practical* question was whether the present state of affairs here would not be found unsatisfactory, and the climate hotter and less healthy than was desirable, or whether the luxuriant indications of opulence and ease I now beheld might not prove to be more captivating than expected, and the climate even more delightfully salubrious than I had dared to anticipate. I watched the lingering sunlight, wrapping the clouds, the mountains, and the sky into one glowing and refulgent scene, with all the enthusiasm of which my soul was capable; but the sun went quietly down, and the supper-bell reminded me of a fresh-caught mackerel. The sun and the land will come again to-morrow, but the mackerel disappeared forever.

Morning did come, and with it came the pilot (black). We entered the "port of silver" (Puerto del Plata). The harbor is a poor one; but if there be one thing on earth deserving the epithet "sublime," it is the surrounding scenery. We anchored, and there awaited the coming of the custom-house officers. The officers came—some white, some colored—and with them Mr. Collins, an American gentleman to whom I was addressed. He received me liberally, invited me to stop with him, promising to show me around the country, introduce me to the General, (black) and do a variety of other things decidedly un-American, but very gentlemanly indeed.

It was Saturday afternoon when we went ashore, and it so happened there was to be a government proclamation. In due time the drum struck up, and down came the standing army, looking for all the world like a parcel of ragamuffin boys playing militia. I counted them, and I think there were four drummers, two fifers, and two lines of soldiers—thirteen in a line. Some were barefooted, others wore shoes; some of their guns had bayonets, and others none. The manner in which they bore them compared with the foregoing suggestions, and so on to the end of this ridiculous scene. Dominicana has a government—so poets have empires.

In passing through the streets one is compelled to observe the non-progressive appearance of everything around him. There lie the unturned stones, just as they were laid a century ago. The houses are generally built one story high, with conical-shaped roofs, for no other reason than that that is the way this generation found them. Mr. Collins, who is a bachelor, lives in an airy two-story house, with a charming verandah running its whole length, cool and delicious, and surrounded by the sweetest fruit-trees outside of Eden. I found myself perpetually exclaiming, "Oh! what beautiful, bright roses!" what this, and what that, until I felt shamefully convicted of my own enthusiastic ignorance. I need not repeat the traveller's story, for the certainty of exposure is sure. Look at a wood-cut and say that you have seen Niagara, but don't read Harper's picture-books and suppose you have any idea of Haytien floral beauty.*

Of course I have not been here long enough to know whether it is a fit place for a man to live in, or for a number to colonize, and I am well aware, when the question of politics comes up, it turns on a very different pivot; but by all that is magnificent, lovely, exquisite, and delicious in its vegetable productions, I do set it down a perfect paradise.

LETTER II

Want of Information — One side of a Question.

There is no school-boy but remembers, when tracing the history of Columbus on his perilous voyage across the sea in search of a new world, how eagerly he watched each favorable indication of bird or sea-weed, and ultimately with what rapture he greeted the joyous cry of land; nor who, looking back through the vista of centuries past, but brings vividly to mind the landing of Columbus, the simplicity of the natives, the cupidity of the Spaniards, and their insatiable thirst for gold. But further than this —further than a knowledge of a few of the most striking outlines of the earlier history of Hayti, or Hispaniola— there is generally known little or nothing; little of the vicissitudes and sanguinary scenes through which the peoples of this island have passed; nothing of the "easily attainable wealth almost in sight of our great commercial cities;" nothing of its sanitary districts peculiarly conducive to longevity. On the contrary, erroneous and exaggerated notions prevail, that because it is not within

---

* When the island was discovered by Columbus, it received from him the name of Hispaniola—"Little Spain." It was afterwards called Santo Domingo; but the original name given it by the natives, and revived by Dessalines, is said to be Hayti. The Haytien territory, however, is but about two-fifths of the island, the greater part being owned by the Dominicans.

a given circle of isothermal lines it must necessarily be fit for the habitation only of centipedes, bugbears, land-sharks, and lizards. Indeed, it has been well said there is perhaps no portion of the civilized world of which the American people are so uninformed; and, in fact, so anomalous and apparently contradictory to the generally received impression does everything appear, that I almost despair of these papers being regarded as other than humorously paradoxical.

I am standing now on the line of 19° 45′ of north latitude, or but 20° 15′ south of the city of New York, and but 3° of longitude east, a distance not greater, I think, than by river from St. Louis to New Orleans, a distance frequently made by steamers within four days, and a distance which may be travelled over on railroads in the States at the rate of three times a week! Yet there are many persons who, were you to speak to them concerning this portion of the American tropics, you would find, regard it as being somewhere away on the coast of Africa, and the voyage hither long and tediously disagreeable. It is in reality but a small pleasure trip.

This is one side; but the great lesson of the world's experience is that there are two sides to every question.

THE OTHER SIDE

On the other hand, it may well be asked, if this be the Eden of the New World, why its flowers should be "born to blush unseen," and its "gems of purest ray" remain hidden in its hills; or, to speak less classically, why the country should lie so long a comparative *terra incognita,* producing generations of indolent men and women, excelling only in superstition, idleness, and profound stupidity. In the "Silver Port," the port in which we entered, vessels get within a quarter of a mile of land; then lighters take the cargo half the remaining distance, and from thence ox-carts convey it to the shore, when a comparatively small outlay of ingenuity, capital, and labor would make it a respectable harbor.

The men generally dress—those that dress at all—in cool white linen, Panama hats, and light gaiter boots. They look nice; but the red-turbaned, often bare-stockinged, loosely-dressed women are shocking.

"Know then this truth, (enough for man to know,)
Virtue alone is happiness below."

Soon after we arrived, a dark, brown-skinned, and as handsome a looking man as I ever saw, came on board as watchman. For my particular benefit, I suppose, the captain inquired if he had a wife; to which he replied, in broken Spanish, "Two—one is not a plenty."

A large portion of the cargo of the vessel in which I came consisted of lumber for the erection of a storehouse. The same vessel will be freighted back with timber of a superior quality. Indeed, the shores are lined with yellow-wood and mahogany; *but it is not sawed.* A gentleman is reported to have built a house in one of the interior towns which would have cost in Northern Ohio about $800, at a cost of $25,000. Inquire why this is so— why this listless inactivity prevails—and you receive the answer, "Well, waat is the use?" or, as Tennyson has it, "Vot's the hods, so long as you're 'appy." The "apathy of despair" has not reached here, but the apathy of stupidity is incurable.

CAUSES OF THE DECLINE OF THE SPANISH COLONY

I am aware that many persons, among them our finest writers on "Civilization—Its Dependence on Physical Circumstances," attribute the cause of the island's decline from its ancient splendor, and the consequent supine indifference of the natives, to the effeminating influences attending all tropical climates; and, without prejudice, I believe such would be very greatly the case in a very large portion of the tropical world; but it is a libel on Hayti and Dominicana. The country is as healthy as Virginia, and, except in its excessive beauty and fertility, resembles much the state of North Carolina. "Nobody dies in Port-au-Platte," they say; but I should be sorry to find it true. I trace the cause in the country's history, as I think the following brief glance will show, for much of which I am indebted to W. S. Courtney, Esq., and his essay on "The Gold Fields of St. Domingo."* We will say the civilized history of the country began with the Spaniards in 1492. The inhabitants, at the time of its discovery by Columbus, were a simple-minded, hospitable, and kind-, hearted people, the fate (unparalleled suffering) of whom I have no disposition to record. The studious reader of American history will shudder at the bare recollection of the predatory scenes and excessively inhuman and bewildering iniquities of which they fell the victims, and which, if perpetrated now in any part of the world, "would send a thrill of horror to the heart of universal man." Montgomery, I think it is, expresses their fate touchingly, and in a nut-shell, thus:

"Down to the dust the Carib people passed,
Like autumn foliage withering in the blast;
A whole race sunk beneath the oppressor's rod,
And left a blank among the works of God!"

The Spanish colonists brought with them, of course, the Spanish language, customs, laws, and religion, which language, customs, and religion prevail to this day. They were exceedingly prosperous through a long series of years. They built palatial residences, cultivated sugar and tobacco farms, erected prodigious warehouses, established assay offices, and worked the mines on a grand but unscientific scale. The mines are supposed to have yielded from twenty-five to thirty millions of dollars per annum,

---

* Wilshire S. Courtney, *The Gold Fields of St. Domingo.* . . .
(New York: A. P. Norton, 1860). H. H. B.

and the exports of sugar and other productions showed a corresponding degree of prosperity.

In about 1630 the island began to decline. The natives had been driven and tortured to the last degree, and the heroic Spaniards began to look around for other countries to conquer, other people to enslave. They discovered Mexico, Peru, and Brazil. The most glowing and captivating accounts went forth of the incalculable wealth of those countries in silver and gold, and multitudes abandoned their homes and haciendas and flocked thitherwards, in the hope of realizing wealth untold. Plantations and mines that had been producing immense revenues were abandoned to waste and desolation, and the population of the island was reduced one half from this one cause alone. Meanwhile, the French had established themselves on the western part of the island, and the present Haytien territory was ceded to France in 1773.

The remaining Spaniards introduced African slaves to supply the place of natives, and with this labor they were enabled to recover somewhat of their ancient thrift. Soon after this, the revolt in the French portion of the island occurred, and many of the Spanish slaves left the territory to join the standard of their revolutionary brethren. Besides this, whenever the French royalists drove the revolutionary forces back into the mountains, and cut off their supplies, the latter entered the Spanish territory, helped themselves to what they needed, destroyed the haciendas, carried off cattle and crops, and if they were resisted, as they sometimes were, they slaughtered the Spaniards as they do hogs in Cincinnati, Ohio, set the cities on fire and left behind a grand but terribly universal ruin.

The history of San Domingo was never completely written, and if it were, would never find a reader. But stand here on these shores, with a rising panorama of half the scences enacted by these revolting and infuriated slaves, and there is not a planter in the Southern United States, who, for all the wealth Peru, Mexico, and St. Domingo could produce, would be willing to return home and remain there over night.

Finally, Dessalines, that extraordinary prince of cutthroats, entered the Spanish territory, slaughtered the French, laid waste the country for leagues, carried off the remaining slaves and so bewildered and astounded the Spanish residents that they gathered up what movable wealth they could and left the country, "some for Mexico, some for Peru, while many returned to Spain."

Such are the principal and to me satisfactory causes which history assigns for the decline of the island's thrift, which had reached an unparalleled degree of prosperity and an unsurpassed grandeur and magnificance, with a rapidity unrivalled in the annals of the world.

SUBSEQUENT HISTORY

For the gratification of your many readers, I will continue this homoeopathic sketch of the island's history up to the present time.

In 1821 the Dominican portion (which embraces about three-fifths of the island, but having, I think, not more than one-fourth of its population) declared itself independent of the Spanish crown, but was shortly after subjugated by Boyer, the President of the Haytien Republic. In 1842 a revolution in Hayti caused Boyer to flee, and Riviere assumed the presidency. Two years after, the Dominicans overpowered Riviere, and on the 27th of February, 1844, reestablished their government, or rather the present government of Dominicana. The main features of their constitution are, that each district or canton choose electors, who meet in preliminary electoral convention, and elect for four years the President and other administrative officers, and a certain number of counsellors, who constitute a congress.

The President, Pedro Santana, is a mixed blood of Spanish and Indian descent, and is emphatically regarded as a most estimable personage. Baez, the former President, is said to be of mixed French and African lineage; in short, there is no difference on account of color.

In 1849, Solouque, the President of Hayti, contrary to the wish of many Haytiens, undertook to conquer the Dominicans, and bring them unwillingly under his despotic sway. He entered the territory with five thousand men, but was met at Las Carreas, and disastrously defeated by General Santana, "with an army of but four hundred men under his command." This is the truth, or history is a lie.

For this brilliant achievement Santana received the title of "Libertador de la Patria," and seems to be admired, comparatively speaking, after the manner of our "liberator" and Father of his country. (Bah!)

But a small portion of the Haytiens, as I have before observed, sympathized with President Solouque in his abortive attempt to carry out the "Democratic" policy of territorial expansion. And when General Geffrard was proclaimed President, it is said the populace demanded pledges that he would not pursue the policy of his predecessor in this regard.

"It is not at all probable that any organized attempts of the Haytiens to recover possession of the Dominican territory will ever again be made; so that henceforth there will be no more annoyances of this sort." Such are the views and opinions of eminent men, who have given this subject some attention;* but in the opinion of the writer, as is generally known, the destiny of the island is union;—one in government, wants, and interest, brought

---

* Within fifteen days a disaffection has been discovered near the Haytien frontiers, supposed to be the work of Solouque. Solouque is an imitator of Napoleon I. Napoleon went to Elba— Solouque to the island of Jamaica.

about by the introduction of the English language, and by other peaceful and benignant mean; such language, wants, and interests to be introduced by the emigration hither of North Americans,—some white, but principally colored. England, France, and many other independent nations of the world, have acknowledged and formed liberal treaties with the weak little Republic, but I hope you do not suppose the government of the United States could be *guilty* of anything that looks like generosity.

God grant that I may never die in the United States of America!

LETTER III

Corpus Christi.

Betwixt midnight and daylight this morning I was lying sleeping and dreaming under the halcyon influences of the lingering land breezes, when suddenly a harmonious sound of partly brass and partly string instrumental music rang upon the air. It appeared just as music always does to any one in a semi-transparent slumber—not quite awake nor yet asleep—when, as everybody knows, it is sweet as love. One boom from the cannon, and I stood square on my feet; and, as it is not very remarkable here to see persons dressed in white, the next moment I was out on the verandah.

There went a jolly crowd, promiscuous enough, but apparently as light-hearted and happy as mortals get to be, and which to a slant-browed contriving Yankee is a poser. They had thus early begun to celebrate what is called *Corpus Christi,* which, according to all fair translation, I should think means Christ's body. But any thing about it after that I am entirely unable to say. It would seem to require a good deal to understand all the Catholic

ceremonies. Talk about their being ignorant! I never
expect to learn so much while I live.

All business houses were closed for the day, and
Dominican, French, American, and other colors were
flying from their respective staffs. Altars were erected in
various streets, with numerous candles burning within,
and bedecked with parti-colored flags and flowers. They
were really prettily and tastefully arranged. In short, it
was an American 4th of July, except this: to each of these
altars marched the throng of people headed by the priest.
The priest said prayers in "Greek." The people *understood,* and all knelt down in the street, men, women, and
children, but of course principally women.

THE FARM OF THE FUGITIVE SLAVE

A party of us went out to see Mr. Smith, a fugitive slave,
whose energy and well-directed enterprise had attracted
some attention heretofore. He is not so fine looking a
man as I expected to see. He is under five and a half feet
in height, limps a little, and is altogether but little in
advance, to use a most contemptible Americanism, of his
"kind of people" in the States. He speaks no Spanish,
and for that matter very little English; but he has a
will of his own, and a determination to do something,
which gives him an advantage over half a dozen persons
who go to school to lose their common sense.

Mr. Smith was a slave in South Carolina; was
brought by sea to Key West, and there hired out to
work for a Republican government. He and some other
of his fellow-slaves, including his wife, took sail-boat, set
sail, and after suffering almost incredibly from sea-sick-
ness and want of food, finally reached New Providence,
which he had previously learned to be an English colony.
He proceeded to declare his intention to become a British
subject, and went to work; but wages being low, he concluded to remove to Dominicana and go to farming. He

purchased a piece of land near the town of Porto Plata, and with the assistance of his "help-mate," (which in this country means a wife,) soon cleared the land of its tropical undergrowth, and planted it in corn and potatoes. In breaking up the ground he used a plow, a startling innovation here, but which produced most salutary results. A neighbor of his has since bought one. So great was the yield of Mr. Smith and his wife's crop that in little more than a year's time they have a house and forty acres of land all paid for, and a new crop worth over five hundred dollars, which will soon be ready for market.

This may not seem very remarkable to any one who has never seen a sand-hill, nor yet been to Canada; but to me it is a miracle. My object in mentioning this fact, however, is, to state that Mr. Smith also planted a few seeds of Sea-Island cotton, the product of which has been sent to New York and pronounced worth 14c per pound. Now, there are numbers of colored men recently from the Southern States skilled in, and some who have made small fortunes by, cultivation of cotton, at perhaps not more than eight or nine cents per pound, when, too, it had to be replanted every year. It produces here without replanting almost indefinitely, but it is safe to say seven years.

The query is this: give half a dozen such men as Smith a cotton-gin ($350), send them out here, and would they not accomplish more for the elevation of the colored race by the successful cultivation of cotton, in eighteen months, than all the mere talkers in as many years?

The meanest thing I have been obliged to do, and the greatest sin I have committed, has been the registering my name as an American citizen. I presented myself to the United States consul (whose son and clerk, by the way, is a mulatto). The nice correspondence of Mr.

Marcy* was produced, not with any evil intent at all, but just to show what indefinable definitions there are between colored and black and white and negroes as American citizens. I should like to find out how a man *knows* he is an American citizen! There are members of Congress who can no more tell this than they can tell who are their fathers.

As for Mr. Corwin's† talk about enforcing the laws, he may thank Heaven if he is not yet arrested as a fugitive slave.

Since the above was written, I understand the courts of Virginia have decided that an Octoroon is not a negro. Now, then, if an octoroon is not a *negro,* is an octoroon a citizen? And if an octoroon is not a negro, is a quadroon a negro?

LETTER IV

First Ride in the Country — Pastorisa Place.

"A yankee is known by the shortness of his stirrups;" so they say here, and I do not know that the criticism is at all too severe. Except Willis and one or two others, who of the Americans know any thing about riding? The Dominicans are good on horseback. In fact, it is their boast that they can ride or march further in two days than Americans want to go in a week. On the other hand, if "Los Yankees" had this country they would soon fix it so that a man could go over it all before the Dominicans

---

* Presumably the reference is to William L. Marcy who had been Secretary of State from 1853 to 1857 and had tried to keep the South happy in interpreting citizenship, but had found it increasingly difficult in the face of growing demands of free blacks for recognition of their rights as citizens while traveling abroad. H. H. B.

† The reference may or may not be to Thomas Corwin, of Kentucky origin, but throughout most of his life a political leader in Ohio. H. H. B.

got breakfast. Señor Pastorisa, (of the firm of Pastorisa, Collins & Co., formerly of St. Thomas,) who married a native, is mounted on a cream-colored horse, (cost $300,) and wears behind him a sword in a silver-gilt case. Every male person wears a sword of some kind, even though it prove to be as useless as an old case-knife. It is an old, superannuated, hundred-years-behind-the-age custom; yet in some instances serves as their Court of Appeals. No one disturbs you, and you are expected to be as well behaved; but if not, the difficulty is generally settled at the sword's point, and there it ends. How magnanimous even is this rude mode of settling disputes when compared to that of the one-sided, blaspheming, defrauding den of thieves called a court of justice in the States! Coming from a land where men kill each other without warning, instead of a sword which I would not know how to use, I buy a pair of holsters for horseman's pistols, throw them across the saddle, and am ready.

Now there may be no pistols in these holsters, of course, but what is the difference so long as they are supposed to be there? I take it as one of the grand lessons which the world's history teaches, that men are far more afraid of supposed and imaginary dangers than of those they know to be real. The number of backsliding sinners and snake-story witnesses are innumerable.

We were now at the base of the St. Mark's mountain, which rises just back of the town of Porto Plata. The so-called road was no road at all. There were little narrow trenches running between the rocks, fit for pack-mules, but scarcely wide enough to allow one's feet to pass. Up the mountain we came *poco a poco*. While passing these rocks the sun poured down with an intensity not previously experienced. But I had never been an alderman, and was not fat enough to melt; indeed, it might as well have shone on a pine knot. Ere long the sun hid behind a cloud, the thunder muttered a little, but pretty soon, is if by way of repentance, there came a restorative shower of tears. (Thank Heaven! the *nigger* question vanquished the sun.) Nothing is so calculated to make a man vain as a mountain shower. You enjoy its ineffable sensations yourself, while below you behold the poor valley fellows sweating in the sun. Or it may be they are drowning wet below, and you basking in the clear sunshine above. Either way, you are bound to rejoice and to look with contempt on the silly ones who make themselves miserable by regretting and whining over things that are in themselves unalterable, and need no change. The wise repine not.

Over the mountain and beside a stream, with limes scattered plentifully around, we stop a moment for refreshment. Lemonade is cheap, one would think; the limes are as free as the water. Had nature furnished the sweetening as well, we should have had a river of lemonade.

Here country settlements begin again, called *estancias,* which, if you will get a blackboard and a piece of chalk, I will explain. Mark off, say four acres of land, clear it up—let the fruit-trees stand, of course—enclose it, but plant nothing therein. In the centre of this piece erect a shanty. This much is called a *conuco.* Now go through the woods, say a mile and a half, clear up four acres more and plant tobacco. The next year or two this will be gone to weeds; you then (not knowing the use of a plow) go another half mile, clear up another piece and plant a new crop. The old place has gone to wreck, the new place is in its vigor; but neither is in sight of the house. This together is called an *estancia,* and I should have said before meant a farm, but it does not mean a farm in English by a good deal.

At this point we leave the "road," and, under full gallop half the while, take through the wood, guided by a dim path which winds over the hills and down the dales with as careless an indiscrimination as ever road was trodden by a prairie herd. L'Ouverture's feats or Putnam's celebrated escape would do to read about, but this was reducing the thing to practice.

Five miles' gallop over a level plain—thirty miles in all—and we have reached Pastorisa Place: it is a perfect Arcadia.

During leisure moments I shall probably look back to this day's ride and to these enchanting scenes as one of the "gilt letter" chapters of my life; but at present, after a bath, the rapidity with which fried plantains, pine-apple syrup, and scorched sweet milk will disappear, would do a dyspeptic Northerner good to see!

The property comes by Señora Pastorisa. She is, perhaps, five-and-twenty. Her eyes are as bright and dark as even Lord Byron could have wished them to be. Her complexion is that of a clear ripe orange. The place is extensive, containing say nineteen thousand acres, in a valley five miles wide, fenced in on either side by a spear of mountains, with a limpid stream running through the centre. Mocking-birds enliven everything; parrots and paroquettes go around in droves, screaming and squawking like a very nuisance. Back of the house is a grove appropriated to honey-bees. They swarm on every log. (There were certainly over one hundred swarms.) Honey is considered of but little value anywhere in the mountains, and is often wasted in the streams, the wax only being preserved. This comes of having pack-mules and goat-paths instead of wagons and wagon-roads.

Señor Pastorisa had informed me before of his desire to quit the town and improve his farm. All he needed was men who understood farming on the American plan. He has a plow, and intends harnessing an ox to-morrow to try the experiment of plowing. Now, it is clear that to plow the ground very successfully he will need at least a yoke of oxen—which he has, all but the yoke. This I would undertake to make, though I never did such a thing in my life, and always had a horror of an ox-yoke, anyway; but lo! there are no tools. So Señor Pastorisa needs hands, but with a very little *a priori* reasoning it will be seen there are other things needed quite as much. One is a road. There is a natural outlet to the valley— there must be. The stream before the door makes towards the Isabella river. The Isabella empties into the sea, of course.

I forgot to Say Señor Pastorisa is "a little tinged"— the handsomest woman in the world.

LETTER V

Valley of the Isabella — Customs of the Natives — Chapter on Snakes — A Call for Dinner.

"Know ye the land where the cypress and myrtle
Are emblems of deeds that are done in their clime;
Where the rage of the vulture, the love of the turtle,
Now melt into sorrow, now madden to crime;
Where the flowers ever blossom, the beams ever shine,
And all save the spirit of man is divine?"—BYRON

There had been one or two invigorating showers previous to our ride down the valley of the Isabella, and so there remained a great deal of slippery clay along the narrow pathways, which paths lay usually on the very verge of some mountain slope, embankment, or more exciting precipice. To have come off with only one or two bones broken, I should have been perfectly satisfied.

We forded the river with impunity, crossed and re-crossed it again, and finally came to as level a bottom plain as wheel ever rolled on. The valley of the Isabella is as handsome as a park.

The river itself is not so large as Longfellow's "Beautiful River," but it is much more deserving the name. Apropos, every old homestead has its particular title, such as the "Mocking-Bird," "Humming-Bird," "Crebahunda," and a variety of others for which there is no adequate translation. The legends attending them are frequently the most exquisite.

Considering, therefore, the remarkable history, exquisite legends, and extraordinary traditions of the country, I am bound to say, should there be sufficient emigration in this direction to produce a poet of the Hiawatha school, I should be sorry for the laurels of Mr. Longfellow. There are one or two parts of "Hiawatha," however, for which I hope to retain a relish.

The houses and cultivation along our way are in keeping with the *estancias* before described. The men are comparatively neat in appearance, find them where you will. The women are frequently good-looking, but seldom spirited. The prevailing question seems to be, How low in the neck can their dresses be worn? and the answer is, Very low indeed! White Swiss is worn as dress, and when seen on a handsome woman is like Balm of Gilead to the wounded eye. The wife does not usually eat at the table with her husband. She sees that his baths are ready, and at times even that his horse is fed, and at meal-times either takes her plate on her lap or awaits the second table. This is not from want of respect on the part of either; it is their stupid custom. Should "los Americanos" ever run a stage-coach up this valley, and two or three of these fellows have to climb on top for the sake of giving one lady an inside seat, they will comprehend somewhat better for whose convenience the world was made.

June 14th.—Señor Pastorisa fell ill to-day, and is now lying in a hammock. This gives me an opportunity to extol the hammock, which is too excellent a thing to pass unnoticed. It consists mainly of a net-work of grass, netted something like a seine, twice the length of a person or more, and fastened at the ends with cords sufficiently strong to hold the weight of any one. These cords are tied to the limb of a tree or the rafters of a house, and there you swing as happy as any baby ever rocked in a tree-top. It is sufficiently light to be carried in saddle-bag, and is altogether indispensable.

The señor's fever is also my excuse for pencilling down notes more minutely than I otherwise should. I can, of course, give you a description of but few things singly. The palm-tree ought to be one. This remarkable tree grows without a limb, smooth and regular as a barber-pole, from forty to sixty feet high. At this point it turns suddenly green, and puts out two or three shoots. Around these grow its berries, which are used for fattening pork. Each of these shoots furnishes monthly a rare peel or skin, which is used for covering houses, for packing tobacco, and for making bath-tubs, trays, and other articles of household furniture. The body of the tree is used for weather-boarding. It rives like a lath, the inside being pithy, somewhat like an elder. Its leaves are twelve feet long, and bend over as gracefully as an arch. In the centre of the top springs out a single blade, like the staff of a parasol. This was made (one would think) for mocking-birds to dance on. The most useful tree in the world, its usefulness is excelled by its own beauty.

The valley of the Isabella is a grove of palms.

One cannot but remark how preposterous are the snake stories which the vulgar relate respecting the West Indies and tropics generally. The world does not contain another thing so brazenly destitute of the least common sense. In all this rambling through the woods, over the hills, and along the streams, the most harmful thing I have seen is a honey-bee—not even a dead garter-snake!

While on board a vessel off the coast one day, a sailor threw overboard a hook and line, and in the course of time caught a young shark. It was as wicked a little thing as I ever saw, and strong as a new-born giant. The sailor struck it over the head with a stick, when it

snapped the hook and flounced around the vessel. In
short, he killed it, and proceeded to dress it for breakfast.
"Going to eat a shark?" I inquired.
"Why not?"
"Good heavens! I thought they were the worst things
in the world."
"You eat duck," said he; "what's nastier than a
duck? Shark's clean—swims in a clean sea."
I afterwards tasted a piece: it was coarse, and the
idea that its mother might some day eat me, made the
thing disgusting; but it learned me a lesson I shall not
very soon forget. An Irishman is afraid to go to America
on account of its frogs; a Frenchman makes a dish of
them. One man eats rats, and another cats.

Now, to suppose there were no reptiles whatever in
the country, or none peculiar to its bays and inlets,
would be simply absurd; and when we get to the coast, I
should be sorry to miss seeing some lazy old crocodile
sunning in the sand. Should it have seven heads, however,
I shall very likely catch it, and send it straight to Bar-
num; but if not, why, as Banks* would the Union, let
the snaky thing slide.

Your "Allergater in de brake" song may do for the
Southern States, with their rhythmetical-and-stolen-from-
the-African-coast slaves; but to apply it to this country
would disgrace the most idiotic "What-is-it" ever im-
ported. Of naturally wild quadruped animals there is
not so much as a squirrel. Birds are without number.

Stanley is himself again! One and a half hours'
ride, two fords of the river, (rising,) and we are at the
mouth of the famous Isabella. The river is here, but the
town of Isabella has passed away forever. The delta is
covered with mahogany timbers; two schooners stand out
in the distance waiting to transport them to Europe; and
with these exceptions—and with these alone, unless it be

---

* Possibly Nathaniel P. Banks, Congressman, Governor of
Massachusetts. H. H. B.

the absence of the Indians—were Columbus to arrive here again to-day, he would not find a particle more of improvement than was found here over three centuries and a half ago. A boat load of oarsmen coming down the river, the captain leading in a song, and all hands joining in the chorus; a splash is heard on the other side of the water, as if broken by a fish or clumsy sea-turtle; but except these sounds a death-like stillness pervades the entire valley.

To get a better view, you must cross the promontory (the northernmost point of the island) to where Columbus first landed. From thence you see the Haytien frontier stretching away in the dim blue distance, and the scene is enchantment.

Over the rocks we go, led by a Spaniard on a little bay mule, that climbs over the cliffs with an agility creditable even for a mountain goat. The señor's horse falters. One misstep, and they both go to eternity!

We are on the beach. My zeal to commemorate the landing of Columbus by gathering a few tiny tinted shells reconciles the señor to sit in the sun and hold my horse for a minute; but I have no doubt he had rather see me as expert at gathering peas or picking up potatoes. "Ah! H.," says he, "leave off writing books and gathering shells; get married, and come to farming." So I will—all but the married.

But you will want to know what, after all, is the matter with the port. It is shallow. Vessels of a hundred tons burthen cannot get within as many rods of a harbor. In fact, the only question is, why a man of Columbus' sense ever stopped there at all. It is not worth the pen and ink it would take to describe it.

CALLED AT THE FIRST HOUSE FOR DINNER
"Come, let the fatted calf be slain," was complied with to the very letter, except that in this instance it happened to be a *goat*. Nevertheless, it was worth the return of any prodigal son.

The largest "señorita" had a dress to make up. It was a piece of light blue delaine, and to her, no doubt, was "superb." She left off assisting the old patriarch, in dressing the goat, walked to the pitcher, took the cocoanut dipper, and filled her mouth with water until her cheeks swelled out like a porpoise's. She then deliberately spirted it into her hands; and this was her mode of washing! She then spreads out her dry goods, admires them a while, folds them up again, and lays them aside.

The four, and even six year old, running about the place, were as innocent of even a shirt as any son of Adam at his coming into the world.

We look out into the open, slab-sided kitchen, and see old and young sitting around on the dirt floor, enjoying a meal of fresh goat, winter squash, and plantain stewed together.

Our dinner is over; we bid these folks good-bye, and pronounce them the happiest set of miserably contented mortals the sun ever shone upon. Man needs excitement; he prays for ease.

We return to Pastorisa Place to spend the Sabbath. Two or three days of rest, and we start fresh again for Porto Cabello.

So ends the week—one at least in my life for which it was worth the trouble to have lived.

LETTER VI

On the way to Porto Cabello — Antille-Americana — Emigration Ordinance.

> "Here in my arms as happy you shall be,
> As halcyon brooding on a winter sea."
> —Dryden

When the saffron sunlight lingers on the fleecy edges of these mountain clouds, there is a singular solemnity and peculiar fascination about them which can not be likened to any thing earthly. More than any thing else, the resemblance is that of a dark mourning-gown, lined with white satin and trimmed with silver tassels.

This reminds me that the sign of mourning here is somewhat novel. It is that of a spotless white kerchief worn on the head—a thing rarely seen, however, for the reason that people in this district rarely die except from sheer old age. There is near us an old man (black) whose entire grey hair and bodily appearance indicate his being at least eighty. His father died only a year ago, and for some time before the aged sire's death it is said that fires had to be kindled for him to sleep by, in order to generate sufficient heat to keep his thin, chilly blood in circulation. His age was beyond his own knowledge.

But the great object of life here seems to be that of eating. The first thing in the morning after leaving your hammock, you are furnished with a dish of aromatic coffee, strong and excellent as a beverage, and as little like the ordinary stuff you get at hotels as pure rich cream is like chalk and water. Bah! think of your dish-water slops, made of parched peas, and supposed to be West India coffee! Oh! nation of Barnums and egregious dupes!

Where circumstances allow it, not an hour in the day passes without something being brought in to be eaten. "This is an alligator pear—must be eaten with salt and pepper." Now it is honey, pineapple, mango, orange, banana, and even a joint of sugar-cane—anything to be eating. You are then expected to eat as hearty a dinner as ought to satisfy a man for a week. Ride a mile and a half and you are asked if you are not hungry. You reply, "No, indeed." Cross the next stream, and "Are you not thirsty?" is asked. Say, "No, indeed" again if you like, and you will be very lucky not to hear your admirable self inelegantly compared to some kind of a goat.

The climate of these mountains seems to be that of

perpetual spring, 88° Fahrenheit being the warmest day we have had so far. I understand, however, that in September the heat is much more oppressive because there are more calms, but never so intolerable as in the changeable latitudes. Sunstroke! You might venture the reputation of half a dozen "speakers" (a trade which is had in the States for the picking of it up) that such a thing as sunstroke would not be felt here until the world has wheeled as many years backward as it has forward.

We are trotting along the way to Porto Cabello. I have given you a description of these valleys before, but passing a grove of *rose-apples* just now, (a fruit highly prized in the West Indies simply for its flavor, the tree being much like that of a lime, and the fruit hollow, something like a May-apple, lustrous as an orange, and flavored precisely as a rose is perfumed,) I could but reflect that if another Eve were to be placed in an earthly garden I should pray that it might be somewhere among the hills of New England, for, doubtless, then she would meet temptation with a masterly resistance; but if placed in such a garden as might be made in this country,— with all the sins of the world before her I fear she would be tempted over again a thousand times.

Stop a moment on an elevated point of a homestead called "Crebehunda;" behold the grand valleys stretching away between the mountain chains until lost in the green-blue sea which the glass shows in the distance. Dodging under branches, going sometimes head-first through the eternal verdure which, if possible, grows even more luxuriant, in this way we ultimately reach Porto Cabello, a place which proves to be, as previously understood, the grandest point for a port of entry on the whole northern coast of the island.

These old Spaniards are all the time saying to me, "My son, you never look pert."

"Perfectly happy, uncle," I reply.

"Look long time away—studying."

"Nothing, uncle—only an American."

"Only an American? Well, what do they different from other people?"

"Lay out towns one day, and build them the next; own lands, and improve them."

Now, this is genuine American talk; whether it will be American practice remains to be seen.

Porto Cabello is now used to some extent as a point of export; but the only reason why it is not used more extensively is, that between this and the valley there is a hill to be crossed, which could be made respectable as a highway by six sturdy hands in as many days. The country is ripening for immigration. Mr. James Redpath, a talented English-American, and a most acute observer, recently traversed a portion of the Haytien territory, and came to the conclusion that the entire island was capable of sustaining 20,000,000 people. There is not upon it probably one million, and of these the greater portion are in Hayti. The Dominican territory, by far the most extensive and desirable, does not contain much over one-fourth of a million, all told.

I say the country is ripening for immigration. The Pike's Peak fever will ere long be exhausted. Then there is, probably, no more promising field for enterprise than this in the entire new world. Most any point could be made to flourish by the opening of good roads. With Porto Cabello this is peculiarly so. Santiago is the principal interior town. It is the proper place for, and was the former capital. It is situated on the river Yaque, which courses La Vega Real, (the Royal Plains,) and contains about 12,000 inhabitants. The trade of Porto Plata is kept alive mainly from this source; but the mountainous road between them, over which nothing can be transported except by piecemeal on horseback, has been well-nigh the ruin of them both. Porto Cabello is sixteen miles west of Porto Plata. It shuns the St. Mark's mountain, and it is fair to suppose that, could communication once be established between this and Santiago, and were there the least facilities here for shipping produce, the trade of the interior would inevitably flow in this direction. As to the shipping interest, it was that which first turned our attention hither; for Porto Plata being an unsafe harbor for the winter, vessels had been known to make this port for safety. There are nine feet of water on the shallowest bar, and this once over there are two quiet bays, in either of which a merchantman could ride without an anchor.

There will be an American settlement up this valley,—the nucleus where I now stand, and this their port of entry. Such a settlement would meet the encouragement of Señor Pastorisa, and, as I have reason to believe, of the natives generally. They have no labor-saving machines, which is, beyond all question, what the country most needs. Think of a community like this getting on without a plow, a cotton-gin, a saw-mill, or anything of the kind. It is, verily, astounding. There is, of course— and it is certainly natural enough—a lingering prejudice against white Americans. This may or may not be overcome; but the natural question is, Are colored men in America competent to infuse the spirit of enterprise which the country demands? *Let the common-sense working-men answer.* My experience with your "leading" would-be-white-imitating upstarts is conclusive.

The route—and a cheap one—is from New York to Porto Plata. Agricultural implements are admitted duty free. I send herewith an important communication, showing the disposition of the government towards immigration. It is easy to see that (if carried into effect) it will mark a new epoch in the country's history.

But before this question is taken into the debating rooms—that is, the pulpits—for discussion, it ought to be understood. If people read Homer's poetic descriptions of imaginary scenery, and come here expecting to find them realized, they will be fully as much disappointed as they deserve. There are times when the clouds rise slowly over the mountain height, with a blazing sun at their backs, when the skies glow with a splendor transcending all conception; yet it is not at all likely they will see these mountains "go bobbing 'round," or "nodding," to suit the convenience of anybody. Must mountains necessarily rest their exalted heads against the bosom of the sky, as if holding constant *tête-à-tête* communion with the stars? If so, there are no mountains here—nothing but potatoe-ridges. Nor will they be blindly dazzled by the excessive resplendence of the sun or moon; nor will the moon make silver out of anything upon which it may happen to shine. Moonshine is moonshine, I suppose, the world over. American poets, however, may be read with impunity.

> "This is the land where the citron scents the gale;
> Where dwells the orange in the golden vale;
> Where softer zephyrs fan the azure skies;
> Where myrtles grow, and prouder laurels rise."

IMMIGRATION ORDINANCE

The following is a translated copy of an important official paper published in San Domingo city, June 9th, and proclaimed in Porto Plata, June 28, 1860:

"Antonio Abad Alfau, General of Division, Vice President of the Republic, and entrusted with the executive power, looking at the necessity which exists for facilitating the execution of the laws concerning immigration, defining the manner of making effective the measures which the government may take for their observance, the council of Ministers having heard, has come to issue the following ordinance:

"A R T . 1.   That there be constituted a Board of Immigration in each capital of a province, and in the qualified ports of Samana and Puerto Plata. These shall be composed of four members named by His Excellency, among those most friendly to the progress of the country, of the Governor of the provincial capital, or the Commandant-at-Arms in the communes, who shall be the president of them. Their secretaries shall also be of said commission.

"A R T . 2. These Boards shall meet at the seat of government in the provincial capital, and in the communes of Puerto Plata and Samana, at the Commandant-at-Arms. For their internal ordering and the more ready fulfillment of that which is assigned them, they shall regulate that which they have to do according to utility, first submitting it for approval to the Minister of the Interior.

"A R T . 3. The functions of the Board are: First, to learn the easiest and cheapest way of bringing immigrants to the country, always communicating everything to the President through the Minister of the Interior. Second, to employ all means leading to the result that there shall only come as immigrants the agricultural class, or those following some craft, profession, or useful form of labor; to get information of lands belonging to the nation most suitable for health and fertility; to have them prepared to furnish to farmers who may not have been able to agree with private individuals under the terms of their contracts; to assign them lodgings and sustenance after their arrival, during a period to be agreed on, and to look after them with all the attention and care which it shall be possible to display; to supply them with tools and other articles of use which it may be decided to furnish to them, and with the first stock of seedcorn for their sowing, taking care that everything be of the best quality; to take care that those who agree with private persons shall be under a contract which insures the fulfilment of that which has been agreed with them; to attend to all things which can give credit to this department as well within as without the Republic.

"ART. 4. The Board shall appoint agents for the furnishing of victuals to those who shall be needy, taking care that in every thing there be exactness, order, and good faith.

"ART. 5. All accounts of expenses which may actually be incurred must be examined and approved by the Board, and submitted to the inspection of the Minister of the Interior.

"ART. 6. The office of member of the Board is honorary, and without pay, and they shall perform their functions two years. Those who perform with zeal and patriotism their trust, will be entitled to the esteem and consideration of their fellow-citizens.

"ART. 7. The present ordinance will be promptly executed by the Ministers of the Interior, Police, and Agriculture.

"Given at St. Domingo City, the capital of the Republic, the 4the day of June, 1860, and the 17th year of independence.

"A. ALFAU

"Countersigned, the Minister Secretary of State, in the departments of justice and education, charged with those of the interior, police, and agriculture.

"JACINTO DE CASTRO."

LETTER VII

Proposed American Settlement — Picture of Life — Tomb of the Wesleyan Missionary.

"Thy promises are like Adonis' garden—
That one day bloomed, and fruitful were the next."
—KING HENRY VI

I have scarcely time to inform you of an American settlement really begun. It is near the sea, not far from Porto Plata, on a large *commonality* or tract of land embracing about twelve square miles, (not twelve miles square,) having a water power running full length. The land being in common is considered of the first importance, for by this means a small outlay of capital—say one hundred dollars—secures to the settler the grazing advantage of the whole tract, where not otherwise in use. This idea was suggested by an eminent gentleman of St. Louis, and has been the custom of early settlements in Spanish colonies for centuries past. It will of course be subdivided whenever desired, each man taking the part he had originally improved. The principal settlers are from Massachusetts, one of whom, a Mr. Treadwell, (colored,) designs establishing a manual-labor school. Another, a Mr. Locke, (white,) who came out for his health, has actually secured a mill site, erected a small shanty, and cleared from twelve to twenty acres of land, as preparatory steps towards building a saw-mill. How happy will be the effect of such enterprise on a non-progressive people you have probably anticipated from what I have previously observed.

The manual-labor school is, without question, the only mode of infusing a tone of morality in the country, or giving a foothold to the Protestant religion. This has been tried. About twenty years ago a society of Wesleyan Methodists established a mission in the town of Porto Plata. The church still lives, and is, by foreigners, comparatively well attended; but they have not converted a single Catholic by preaching from that day to this. The reason is, the Catholics will not go to hear them. Yet, for the benefits of an education, about one hundred and fifty children were sent regularly to school, and there, by the "infidel" teachings of the Wesleyans, they soon learned to distrust the ceremonies of their mother church. Unfortunately, about two years since this school was discontinued, and, having succeeded in weaning the people from positive Catholicism without yet embracing the Protestant religion, it seems to have left them with a general belief in every thing, which is, as I take it, the nearest point to a belief in nothing.

The country around Porto Plata is owned almost entirely by the Catholic church, being leased, through the government, at reasonable rates to such persons as desire to settle thereupon; but by establishing a school at a distance of seven miles, as above indicated, it would be entirely free from all such influences. An English missionary is soon to come over from one of the neighboring islands to give the location his personal inspection.

The sea view is divine. Along the shallow edges the rippling waves appear brightly green—greener than the trees—while beyond this, where the water deepens, the hue is a pearly purple—purer purple than a grape. In fact, the earth does not contain a comparison for the tranquil beauty of this transparent sea. Some hours ago I thought to sketch it for you, lest it should prove, like so many other things, too fine to last; but so it continued hour after hour, and until the sun nestled in its very heart.

So much for the future settlement. It may be called "Excelsior," but at present I will call it "Crebahunda."

This cool morning air nearly chills me. You take a bath and retire to bed at night with only a thin linen sheet spread over you. In the morning you are chilled, and resolve to sleep hereafter under more covering; but, of course, when night comes again you do not need any more.

Not a morning, my dear H., do I look upon these fields of living green but that I think of you and your daily routine of office duties. I take a seat beneath one of these forbidden-fruit trees while the land breeze is freighting the valley with perfume, the sun just peeping over the hills, and the white mists, beautiful as a bridal veil, slowly rising up the mountain green; now listening to the voice of a favorite mock-bird, and then to the softer cooings of a mourning-dove. A strange-looking little hummy perches on the first dead limb before me. Parrots squawk, and a dozen blackbirds chime one chorus, while other varieties chirp and trill. The whole scene is Elysian. Then along comes a sparrow-hawk, and choo-ee! choo-ee! choo-ee! off they all go, helter-skelter.

Of whom is this a picture? You are toiling away, arranging rude manuscripts, at times almost discouraged, but still toiling on in your close, hot rooms—and this for the good of your race. Well, Heaven grant they may thank you for it, and save you from crying at last, "Choo-ee! choo-ee!" But, ah!—even worse than that—I am afraid the sparrow-hawks will catch you! With me, the end of every thing is that of the birds—a melancholy aggravation. I have been entranced by these morning scenes but a passing short while, and will soon be compelled to leave them and take a lonely ride to the coast, thence to depart for a season. I therefore stuff my saddle-bags with oranges and cinnamon-apples, as I think this is wiser than weeping.

An absence of precisely four weeks, and we are once again in sight of Porto Plata. "The moon is up, and yet it is not night." Some kind of a holiday being at hand, men, women, and children are riding to and fro up and down the streets on donkeys, mules, and ponies of every description. The scene is truly picturesque. I could but remark to my friend the Protestant exhorter, the grandeur of the evening, to which he replied, "A man that could find fault with this climate would find fault with Paradise." I do not believe him, however, for whether the day and night trips along the coast have been too much for me or not, I have certainly got the chill-fever.

This morning, July 7th, I visited the tomb of the Wesleyan missionary to whose labors here I have before referred. The following inscription will furnish the data to such of your readers as are interested in the history of such missions:

IN MEMORY

OF THE

REV. WM. TOWER

WHO WAS BORN AT HORNCASTLE,
LINCOLNSHIRE, ENGLAND, ON
THE 12TH FEBRUARY, 1811, AND
ENTERED UPON
THE MISSIONARY WORK OF EVANGE-
LIZING THIS ISLAND IN
1838.
HE LABORED ON THIS STATION FOURTEEN
YEARS AND A HALF.
HE WAS BELOVED BY ALL WHO KNEW HIM; AND
DIED ON THE 25TH OF AUGUST,
1853,
UNIVERSALLY REGRETTED.

LETTER VIII

Summary of Staples, Exports, and Products.

"I came across a copy of Rousseau this morning," said an American scholar, whom we had met before; and he added, "I should not have been more surprised had I seen it drop out of the clear sky."

There are but very few books in Dominicana of any kind, and no reliable statistics. The government on the south side of the island appoints custom-house officers on the north side, allowing them little or nothing for their services. The consequence is, these officers pay themselves out of the import duties, and hence few returns are accurately made.

In the essay on the "Gold Fields of St. Domingo,"*

---

* Published by A. P. Norton, New York.

to which I have previously referred, I find the following summary of staples, exports, and products, which, while it is but little more than the reader will have already gathered, may serve at least to confirm what has been said:

"The chief products of the Dominican part of the island are now mahogany, tobacco, indigo, sugar, hides, bees-wax, cocoa-nuts, oranges, lemons, some coffee and some fustic, satin and many other kinds of wood; but the trade in those articles now is not very considerable. There is a vast quantity of *mahogany* in the territory, standing in groves on the mountains and the plains, and scattered over the valleys and along the rivers and streams. The best mahogany in the West Indies grows on this island. Some of these groves and trees are truly magnificent, growing straight and to a great height. The best is now found inland, as it has been nearly all already stripped off the coasts and cut away from near the mouths of the principal rivers and around the bays, where it was more accessible and of easier and cheaper carriage to market. It has been extensively used for building purposes by the inhabitants of the cities, more especially by those of the interior, the lumber now used in the coast cities being carried thither from the States, and exchanged for mahogany and other products. It is only of late years that the best mahogany cuts have begun to come to market, as heretofore they were carried to Europe, where they brought a better price.

"*Tobacco* is now one of the principal exports. But little of it, however, finds its way to this market. There is a large quantity of it raised by the residents on the Spanish part of the island, particularly about Santiago, on the Royal Plains, and in the neighborhood of Maccrere. It is brought down in bales or ceroons on mules to Port Platte, and shipped on board Dutch bottoms to Holland and the Germanic states. There is also some cultivated about St. Domingo City and around the Bay of

Samana. But the cultivation and traffic in this commodity compared with what it might be, were those fertile plains and rich savannahs settled by an industrious and enterprising people, is scarcely as a drop to the bucket. There are regions in the territory where tobacco can be grown equal to the best Havana brands, and, on account of the fecundity of the soil, with even much less labor.

"There are still some good *sugar* plantations in the Dominican territory, chiefly about St. Domingo City and to the west as far as Azua, but they are 'few and far between.' The best sugar is now produced in the region about Azua and Manuel, and is of a very superior quality. The country people cultivate and manufacture, each on his own account, and, in his small way, pack it in ceroons and carry it down to the coast on mules. Indeed, the term 'cultivate' is not appropriately used in this connection, as the cane grows up wild and spontaneously from season to season, and from year to year in many places, and the inhabitants have nothing whatever to do but cut and grind it in wooden mills and boil day after day. The writer is not informed that they use the sugar-mills in use in other sugar-growing countries in their operations. It is easy to conceive what a source of incalculable wealth the culture of this staple there would become, if in the hands of a skilful and enterprising population.

"The trade in *hides,* compared with other products, is quite important, which arises from the fact that a majority of the population pursue grazing for a livelihood, and the rapidity with which stock increases and the little care required in preserving it. Owing to the heat and abundant oxygen which the atmosphere contains, the flesh of the beef, unless properly salted and cured, keeps but a day or two, so that the inhabitants are obliged to kill almost every other day. This now keeps up and supplies the traffic. Perhaps three-fifths of the population of the interior country and towns are now engaged in grazing.

"Compared also with other staples, the trade in *bees-wax* is considerable. The island producing the greatest quantity and variety of flowering plants, shrubs, and trees, bees exist there in incalculable and immense swarms. The prairies of the West in June furnish no parallel to the flowers that perpetually unfold on these mountains, plains, and valleys. The writer has been informed by a gentleman who recently visited Dominica [Dominicana], that so strong and rank was the odor from the flowers in passing over the Royal Plains, that it so jaded his olfactories as to cause his head to ache, and almost made him sick. The swarms build in the rocks, in the trees and logs, under the branches, and even on the ground. Those who pursue this branch of business collect the deposits in tubs, wash out the honey in the brooks by squeezing the combs, and afterwards melt the wax into cakes, or run it into vessels preparatory to carrying it to market. Those engaged in this vocation are chiefly women. The trade in this article, however, bears no proportion to its production and abundance. They have recently begun to save some of the honey, and a small quantity of it has found its way to this market. The reason why it has not been hitherto saved is owing to the great cost of vessels to collect it in, as wooden-ware of all kinds has to be taken there from the States.

"There are some exports of *cocoa-nuts, oranges, lemons, limes,* and other fruit, all of which are both cultivated and grow wild in vast abundance on the island, and are not excelled by any in the Antilles, or on the Spanish main. The labor necessary to collect them, prepare them for shipment, and carry them to the ports is not there. From this cause, indeed, the whole Spanish end of the island languishes in sloth, and its transcendent wealth goes year after year incontinently to waste.

"There is some *coffee,* which grows wild in abundance through the island and on the mountains, and is collected and shipped. After the abandonment of the coffee plantations, the trees continued to grow thick on them, and finally spread into the woods and on to the mountains, where they now grow wild in great quantities. Lacking the proper culture, its quality is not the best, but the climate and soil is capable of producing it unexcelled by any in Porto Rico or any of the West Indies or Brazil. The writer is informed, however, that there are a few coffee plantations under culture about St. Domingo City. The labor of cultivating coffee and sugar in Dominica [Dominicana], with all the modern appliances of civilization, would be absolutely insignificant compared with the rich returns it would bring the planter.

"In addition to the staples and exports above-mentioned, the island produces a vast number of other valuable commodities, among which we may make notable mention of its lumber and different varieties of valuable wood other than mahogany. The pitch or yellow pine grows in vast abundance at the head of the streams and on the mountains, dark and apparently impenetrable forests of which cover their sides and tops. This lumber, with very little expenditure of labor and capital, could be brought down the streams during their rises almost any month in the year, to the principal cities. When the reader is made acquainted with the stubborn fact that all the lumber used on the north side of the island, except the little mahogany that is sawed there and at and about St. Domingo City, is carried there at great cost from the States, and sold at a price fabulous to our lumber-dealers here, he will measurably comprehend the undeveloped resources of Dominica [Dominicana] in that interest alone. Pine lumber sells at Port Platte for $60 per thousand feet. It has then to be carried back to Santiago, Moco, and La Vega on mules, where it sells for $100 per thousand, while those mountains and the banks of their streams stand thickly clothed with it, in its majestic and sublime abundance! There is but one saw-mill on the Spanish end of the island near St. Domingo City, and that not now in operation. They saw by hand a little mahogany at a cost of 80 cents a cut, ten feet long; and when an individual wishes to build a house at Santiago, Moco, La Vega, Cotuy, or any of the interior towns, he has to begin to collect his lumber a year beforehand! . . . In consequence of this scarcity and cost of lumber, those of smaller means build their floors of brick and flags, and roof their houses with the same material or with the leaf of the palm-tree. Besides the pine, there is the oak, the fustic and satinwoods, compache, and an indefinite variety of others. Some of the hardest and most durable vegetable fibre in the world is to be found on the island."

It may appear somewhat strange to the reader that mahogany should be used for building purposes, but so it is. The art of veneering is but little known, house furniture consisting generally of solid mahogany.

Republic of Hayti

LETTER IX

Historical Sketch — General Description Previous to 1790.

"Think not that prodigies must rule a state—
That great revulsions spring from something great."

I have given you Dominicana as a garden of poetry and the home of legendary song. Well, Hayti is a land of historical facts, and the field of unparalleled glory. Consulting one day with Mr. Redpath, the talented author of the series of letters to which I have previously referred, he suggested the impossibility of any one forming even a comparatively correct opinion respecting affairs in Hayti, without being guided by a sketch of the country's previous history. Confessedly, therefore, much as his letters were appreciated by the readers of the *Tribune* he had not done the Haytiens simple justice. Since nothing could be so highly interesting, be it mine and the *Anglo-African's* to undertake what the *Tribune* and its correspondent failed to supply. The following compilation will be taken from Rainsford's, St. Domingo, and Edwards' and Coke's histories of the West Indies, but principally, and when not otherwise marked, from Coke.*

There is nothing low or cowardly in the history of Hayti. Notwithstanding their conquests on the main land, the Spaniards were wont to regard it as the parent colony and capital of their American possessions. The buccaneers of Tortuga, however much they may have

---

* See introduction for bibliographic information. H. H. B.

suffered or have been feared, can not be said to have ever been really conquered. In fact, by whomsoever settled, the country has shown on uninterrupted record of pride and independence. I regard this as an honor to begin with.

The history of Hayti begins with the buccaneers, a company of French, English, and Germans, driven from their homes in the neighboring islands by the haughty arrogance of the Spaniards, in 1629. These men, collected on the shores of Tortuga, vowed mutual fidelity and protection to each other, but eternal vengeance against their persecutors. How well they kept their word has passed into a proverb.

In 1665 the court of Versailles, observing a beautiful country of which some of its subjects had taken an actual though accidental possession, took the fugitive colony under its protection. It was not difficult for the French government to see that the island was in value equal to an empire, and it was therefore determined to enhance its interests with all possible speed. The first care was to select a governor who should be equal to the difficult task of humanizing men who had become barbarians; which important task was committed to D'Ogerton, a gentleman of Anjou.

Hitherto not a single female resided in the settlement, to supply which deficiency was the governor's first care. With this view he sent immediately to France, and many women of reputable character were induced to embark. From this time the prosperity of the colony fairly begins.

The personal fame of D'Ogerton drew many who had suffered persecution at home to flee for safety to an asylum which his lenient measures had established in Hayti, among whom was one Gobin, a Calvinist, who, upon his arrival, (1680,) erected a house on the Cape, and prevailed on others to join him in his retreat. Time added to their numbers, and the conveniences of the situation justified their choice. As the lands became cleared and the value of its commodious bay became known, both inhabitants and shipping resorted to the spot, and raised the town of Cape François to a degree of elegance, wealth, and commercial importance which in 1790 scarcely any city in the West Indies could presume to rival.

Considered in itself, the situation of the town is not to be commended. It stands at the foot of a very high mountain which prevents the inhabitants from enjoying the land breezes, which are not only delicious but absolutely necessary to health. It also obstructs the rays of the sun, causing them to be reflected in such a manner as to render the heat at times almost insupportable. On one side of the town, however, is an extensive plain, containing, perhaps, without any exception, some of the finest lands in the world. The air is temperate, though the days and nights are constantly cool. In short, it is another Eden. "Happy the mortal who first taught the French to settle on this delicious spot."

The situation of Port au Prince, to which place the seat of government has been transferred, seems to have been unfortunately selected. It is low and marshy, and the air is impregnated with noxious vapors, rendering it extremely unwholesome. To this day it is commonly regarded as the graveyard of American seamen. In 1790 it had also reached an eminent degree of prosperity, and contained 14,754 inhabitants, of whom 2,754 were white, 4,000 free people of color, and the remainder slaves. So, also, near Port au Prince is a fertile plain called Cul de Sac. The mountains surrounding it possess a grateful soil, and are cultivated even to their summits. The value of such lands is at present from ten to twenty dollars per acre.

The town of St. Mark's, near which the last body of colored emigrants from America have settled, is somewhat more advantageously situated. It lies on the northern shore of the bay, on the point of an obtuse angle formed by the margin of the rocks and waves. Hills encircle it in the form of a crescent, the points of which unite with the sea, and, while they afford it shelter, leave it open to the breezes of the ocean, which become the springs of health.

The land which the French had brought under cultivation previous to the revolution was devoted mostly to the cultivation of sugar, coffee, indigo, and chocolate. It is said that Hayti alone produced as much sugar at this time as all the British West Indies united. The prodigious productions of little more than two million acres of land were as follows: brown sugar, 93,773,300 lbs.; white sugar, 47,516,351 lbs.; cotton, 7,004,274 lbs.; indigo, 758,628 lbs. But great as this product may appear, it by no means gives the entire amount, the quantity of tanned hides, spirits, &c., being equally immense.

Immorality and irreligion everywhere prevailed, worse even than at present, if we are to judge from a poem written about that time. The West Indies would seem to be peculiarly conducive to this species of iniquity:

"For piety, that richest, sweetest grant,
Of purest love blest super-lunar plant,
Is here neglected for inferior good,
Torn from the roots, or blasted in the bud.
Soft indolence her downy couch displays,
And lulls her victims in inglorious ease,
While guilty passions to their foul embrace
Seduce the daughters of the swarthy race."

This brings us to the consideration of the all-important subject called in America the "negro question," but which is, nevertheless, the immortal question of the rights of man.

The inhabitants of Hayti consisted of 540,000 souls, and were divided into three distinct classes—the whites, the slaves, and the mulattoes and free blacks. The term mulatto comprehended all shades between whites and negroes. The whites conducted themselves as if born to command, and the blacks, awed into submission, yielded

obedience to their imperious mandates, while the mulattoes were despised by both parties.

The freedom they enjoyed was rather nominal than
real. On reaching a state of manhood each became liable
to serve in a military establishment, the office of which
was to arrest runaway slaves, protect travellers on the
public roads, and, in short, to "mount a three years'
guard on the public tranquillity." To complete their
degradation, they were utterly disqualified from holding
any office or place of public trust. No mulatto durst assume the surname of his father; and to prevent the revenge which such flagrant and contemptible injustice
could hardly fail to excite, the law had enacted that if a
free man of color presumed to strike a white man, *his
right arm should be cut off*. In fact, they were not much
above the condition of the free blacks in the United
States. "On comparing the situation of these two classes
of men"—the slaves and the nominally free—says Coke,
"it is difficult to say which was the most degraded. The
social difference was, without doubt, very great, but in
the aggregate must have been about the same."

Such was the state of affairs previous to 1790. What
they have been subsequently remains to be seen. The
whip of terror never yet made a friend. It may prevent
men from being avowed enemies for a while, but it usually makes a deeper impression upon the heart than upon
the skin. The heart is nearest the seat of recollection,
and will stimulate to revenge for a long time after the
wound has been inflicted, as the reader of the following
pages will abundantly attest.

"Time the Avenger! unto thee I lift
My hands and eyes and heart, and crave of thee a gift."

LETTER X

Affairs in France — The Case of the Mulattoes — Terrible
Fate of Ogé and Chavine.

It was towards the close of the year 1788 that the revolutionary spirit which had been fermenting among the French people from the conclusion of the American war first manifested itself in the mother country; and although that extraordinary event convulsed the empire in every part, in no place was the shock so great as in Hayti.

The mulattoes, notwithstanding their oppression and degradation, it should have been observed, were permitted to enjoy property, including slaves, to any amount, and many of them had actually acquired considerable estates. By these means the most wealthy had sent their children to France for education, just as many are now sent to Oberlin, in which place they supported them in no small degree of grandeur.

It happened about this time that a considerable number of these mulattoes were in Paris, among whom was Vincent Ogé. This young man entered into the political questions relative to the people of color, which were then violently agitated, and became influenced with a conflict of passions at the wrongs which he and his degraded countrymen were apparently destined to endure. His reputed father was a white planter, of some degree of eminence and respectability, but he had been dead for years. Ogé was about 30 years of age; his abilities were far from being contemptible, but they were not equal to his ambition, nor sufficient to conduct him through that enterprise in which he soon after engaged. Supported in Paris in a state of affluence, he found no difficulty in associating with La Fayette, Gregorie, and Brissot, from whom he learned the prevailing notion of equality, and into the spirit of which he incautiously entered with all the enthusiasm and ardor natural to the youthful mind when irritated by unmerited injuries; and he determined to avenge his wrongs.

Induced to believe that all the mulattoes of Hayti were actuated by the same high-minded principle, he sacrificed his fortune, prepared for hostilities, and sailed to join his brethren in Hayti.

What was Ogé's disappointment when, after evading the vigilance of the police and secretly succeeding in reaching these shores, he found no party prepared to receive him, or willing to take up arms in their own defence! It probably might have been said of him also, *"His heart is seared."*

About two hundred were at length prevailed upon to rally around his standard; and with this inadequate force he proceeded to declare his intentions, and actually dispatched a note to the governor to that effect.

In his military arrangements his two brothers were to act under him, and with one Mark Cravine, as lieutenants. Ogé and his brothers were humane in their dispositions, and averse to the shedding of blood; but with Chavine the case was totally different.

Ferocious, sanguinary, and courageous, he began his career with acts of violence which it was impossible for Ogé to prevent.

Finally the brothers of Ogé joined Chavine in his petty depredations. White men were murdered as accident threw them in their way. The mulattoes, when they could not be induced to join them, were treated with every species of indignity; and one man in particular, who excused himself from joining them on account of his family, was murdered, together with his wife and six children.

The inhabitants of Cape François, alarmed at these

outrages which they imagined to be committed by a far more formidable body of revolters than really existed, immediately took measures for their suppression.

A detachment of regular troops invested the mulatto camp, which, after making an ineffectual resistance in which many were killed, was entirely broken up. The whole troop dispersed. Ogé and his officers took refuge in the Spanish part of the island. The principal part of their ammunition and military stores immediately fell into the hands of the victors.

The triumphs of the whites over the vanquished insurgents were such that they proceeded from victory to insult. The lower orders especially discovered such pointed animosity against the mulattoes at large that they became seriously alarmed for their personal safety, and many regretted not having joined the now vanquished party.

Urged by fatal necessity many resorted to arms, so that several camps were formed in different parts of the colony far more formidable than that of Ogé. At this time RIGAUD, the mulatto general, makes his appearance, declaring that no peace would be permanent "until one class of people had exterminated the other."

In the midst of these commotions which presaged an approaching tempest, PEYNIER, the governor, resigned his office in favor of general Blanchelande. The first step of the latter was directed towards the unfortunate Ogé. The demand made on the Spanish governor for his arrest was peremptory and decisive. Twenty of Ogé's followers, including one of his brothers, were speedily hung; but a severer fate awaited Ogé and Chavine. They were condemned to be broken alive, and were actually left to perish in that terrible condition on the wheel.

Chavine, the hardy lieutenant, met his destiny with that undaunted firmness which had marked his life. He bore the extremity of his torture with an invincible resolution, without betraying the least symptom of fear, and without uttering a groan at his excruciating sufferings.

With Ogé the case was widely different. When sentence was passed upon him his fortitude abandoned him altogether. He wept; he solicited mercy in terms of the most abject humility; but in the end he was hurried to execution, and left to expire in the most horrid agonies.

Previous to this the National Assembly in France, which had originally declared "That all men are born free, and continue free and equal as to their rights," had to contradict this in order to pacify the planters, and to declare it was not their intention to interfere with the local institutions of the colonies.

It so happened, however, that with this decree they also transmitted to the governor a chapter of instructions, one of the articles of which expressed this sentiment: "That every person of the age of twenty-five and upwards, possessing property or having resided two years in the colony and paid taxes, should be permitted to vote in the formation of the colonial assembly." It was like the Dred Scott decision of the United States, for the question immediately arose whether the term "every person" included the mulattoes.

It was just at this time that intelligence of the tragical death of Ogé, who had been previously well known in Paris, reached that city. The public mind was instantly inflamed against the planters almost to madness, and for some time those in the city were unable to appear in public, either to apologize for their brethren or defend themselves. To keep alive that resentment which had been awakened, a tragedy was founded on the dying agonies of Ogé, and the theatres of Paris conveyed the tidings of his exit to all classes of people.

Brissot and Gregorie, two well-known reformers, availing themselves of this auspicious moment, brought the case of the mulattoes before the National Assembly. This was early in May, 1791. The eloquence displayed by Gregorie on this occasion was most marvellous, enforced by such facts as a state of slavery and degradation rarely fails to produce, and the whole finished by an affecting recital of the death of Ogé.

Amid the ardor with which he pleaded the cause of the mulattoes, a few persons attempted to stem the torrent by predicting the ruin of the colonies. *"Perish the colonies,"* exclaimed Robespierre in reply, "rather than sacrifice one iota of our principles." The sentiment was reiterated amid the applauses of an enthusiastic Senate, and the National Assembly, on the 15th day of May, decreed that the people of color born of free parents should thenceforth have all the rights of French citizens; that they should have votes in the choice of representatives, and be eligible to seats both in the parochial and colonial assemblies.

The colonial representatives no sooner heard that these decisive steps were taken than they declared their office useless, and resolved to decline any further attempts to preserve the colonies.

The colonists who resided in the mother country heard the decree with indignation and amazement. But in the island, as soon as it became known, the planters sunk into a state of torpor, and appeared for a moment as if petrified into statues. All local feuds between the whites were immediately suspended, and all animosities swallowed up by what appeared to them an evil of unparalleled magnitude. The civic oath was treated with contempt; tumult succeeded subordination; proposals were made to hoist the British colors; and resolutions crowded on resolutions to renounce at once all connection with a country that had placed the rights of the mulattoes on an equal footing with their own.

The mulattoes, who became criminal from their color, were obliged to flee in every direction. Their homes afforded them no protection. They were threatened with shooting in the street; and thus menaced by destruction, they began to arm in every direction.

The governor beheld this commotion with palsied solicitude. He foresaw the evils that must burst upon the colony, without having it in his power to apply either a preventive or a remedy.

But a far more awful mine, surcharged with combustibles, and destined to appall all parties, was at that moment on the very eve of an explosion.

LETTER XI

A Chapter of Horrors (which the delicate reader may, if he pleases, omit).

"Out breaks at once the far-resounding cry—
The standard of revolt is raised on high."

Among the various transactions which had taken place, both in the island and in France, little or no attention had been paid to the condition of the slaves. It is true an abolition society had been early established in Paris, called the "Friends of the Blacks," (*Amis des noirs.*) Their sufferings had also been used to give energy to a harangue, or to enforce the necessity of general reformation, but their situation was passed over by the legislative assemblies as a subject that admitted of no redress.

These, sensible of their condition, numbers, and powers, resolved, amid the general confusion, to assert their freedom and legislate for themselves. They had learned from the contentions of both their white and colored masters that violence was necessary to prosperity. Such measures they adopted; and no sooner adopted than they were carried into effect.

It was early on the morning of August 23, 1791, that

a confused report began to circulate through the capital that the negroes were not only in a state of insurrection, but that they were consuming with fire what the sword had spared. A report so serious could not fail to spread the greatest alarm. It was credited by the timid, despised by the fearless, but was deeply interesting to all. Pretty soon the arrival of a few half-breathless fugitives confirmed the melancholy news; they had just escaped from the scene of desolation and carnage, and hastened to the town to beg protection and to communicate the fatal particulars. From these white fugitives (the scale had turned) it was learned that the insurrection was begun by the slaves on a plantation not more than nine miles from Cape François.

There, it appeared, in the dead of night, they had assembled together and massacred every branch of their master's family that fell in their way. From thence they proceeded to the next plantation, where they acted in the same manner, and augmented their number with the slaves whom the murder of their master had apparently liberated. And so on they went, from plantation to plantation, recruiting their forces in proportion to the murders they committed, and extending their desolations as their numbers increased.

From the plantation of M. Flaville they carried off the wife and three daughters, and three daughters of the attorney, after murdering him before their faces. In many cases the white women were rescued from death with the most horrid intentions, and were actually compelled to suffer violation *on the mangled bodies of their dead husbands, friends, or brothers, to whom they had been clinging for protection.*

The return of daylight, for which those who had escaped the sword anxiously waited, to show them the full extent of their danger, was anticipated by the flames that now began to kindle in every direction. This was the work of but a single half night. The shrieks of the inhabitants and the spreading of the conflagration, occasionally intercepted by columns of smoke which had begun to ascend, formed the mournful spectacle which appeared through a vast extent of country when the day began to dawn.

It was now obvious that the insurrection was general, and that the measures of the revolted slaves had been skilfully preconcerted, on which account the revolt became more dangerous. The blacks on the plantation of M. Gallifet had been treated with such remarkable tenderness that their happiness became proverbial. These, it was presumed, would retain their fidelity. So M. Odelac, the agent of the plantation, and member of the General Assembly, determined to visit them at the head of a few soldiers, and to lead them against the insurgents. When he got there he found they had not only raised the ensign of rebellion, but had actually erected for their standard THE BODY OF A WHITE INFANT, *which they had impaled on a stake*. So much for happy negroes and contented slaves! Retreat was impossible. M. Odelac himself was soon surrounded and murdered without mercy, his companions sharing the same fate—all except two or three, who escaped by instant flight only to add their tale to the list of woes.

The governor proceeded immediately to put the towns in a proper state of defence; and all the inhabitants were, without distinction, called upon to labor at the fortifications. Messengers were despatched to all the remotest places, both by sea and land, to which any communication was open, to apprise the people of their danger, and to give them timely notice to prepare for the defence. Through the promptitude with which the whites acted, a chain of posts was instantly established and several camps were formed.

But the revolt was now found to be even greater than imagined. The slaves, as if impelled by one common instinct, seemed to catch the contagion without any visible communication. Danger became every day more and more imminent, so much so that an embargo was laid on all the shipping, to secure the inhabitants a retreat in case of the last extremity. Among the different camps which had been formed by the whites were one at Grande Riviere and another at Dondon. Both of these were attacked by a body of negroes and mulattoes, and a long and bloody contest ensued. In the end the whites were routed and compelled to take refuge in the Spanish dominions. Throughout the succeeding night carnage and conflagration went hand in hand, the latter of which became more terrible from the glare which it cast on the surrounding darkness. Nothing remained to counteract the ravages of the insurgents but the shrieks and tears of the suffering fugitives, and these were usually permitted to plead in vain.

The instances of barbarity which followed are too horrible for description; nor should we be induced to transcribe any portion of them, were it not that many persons regard such statements as mere assertions unless accompanied by a record of the unhappy facts. The recital of a few, however, will set all doubts forever at rest.

"They seized," says Edwards, "a Mr. Blenan, an officer of the police, and, having nailed him alive to one of the gates of his plantation, chopped off his limbs one by one with an axe."

"A poor man named Robert, a carpenter, by endeavoring to conceal himself from the notice of the rebels, was discovered in his hiding place, and the negroes declared that he *should die in the way of his occupation;* accordingly they laid him between two boards, and deliberately sawed him asunder."

"All the white and even the mulatto children whose fathers had not joined in the revolt were murdered without exception, frequently before their eyes, or while clinging to the bosoms of their mothers. Young women of all ranks were first violated by whole troops of barbarians, and then, generally, put to death. Some of them, indeed, were reserved for the gratification of the lust of the leaders, and others had their eyes scooped out with a knife."

"In the parish of Timbe, at a place called the Great Ravine, a venerable planter, the father of two beautiful young ladies, was tied down by the savage ringleader of a band, who ravished the eldest daughter in his presence, and delivered over the youngest to one of his followers. Their passions being satisfied, they slaughtered both the father and the daughters."

"M. Cardineau, a planter of Grande Riviere, had two natural sons by a black woman. He had manumitted them in their infancy, and treated them with great tenderness. They both joined the revolt; and when their father endeavored to divert them from their purpose by soothing language and pecuniary offers, they took his money, and then stabbed him to the heart."

Amid the worst of these scenes Mr. Edwards records that solitary and affecting instance wherein a *soft-hearted* slave saved the lives of his master and family by sending them adrift on the river by moonlight.* This is generally admitted to have been the *Washington* of Hayti, Toussaint L'Ouverture.

At this time, also, the mulatto chiefs, actuated by different motives, not only refused to adopt such horrid measures, but particularly declared their only intention in taking up arms was to support the decree of the 15th of May, which had acknowledged their rights, of which the whites had been endeavoring to deprive them, and proposed to lay down their arms provided the whites acknowledged them as equals.

The white inhabitants gladly availed themselves of an overture which, though it pressed hard on their ambition, afforded a prospect for deliverance from impending

---

* For a beautiful description of this affecting scene, see Whittier's "Toussaint L'Ouverture."

danger. A truce immediately took place, which they denominated a *concordat*. An act of oblivion was passed on both sides over all that had passed, the whites admitting in all its force the decree giving equality to the mulattoes. The sentence passed upon Ogé and the execution of it the *concordat* declared to be infamous, and to be "held in everlasting execration." So much for Ogé.

Both parties now appeared to be equally satisfied, and a mutual confidence took place. Nothing remained but to induce the mulattoes to join the whites in the reduction of the negroes, now in a most formidable state of insurrection. To this the mulattoes consented. New troops were introduced from France. The whites were elated; and perfect tranquillity stood for a moment on the very tiptoe of anticipation.

But the great lesson of the revolution was speedily to be learned. The hurricane of terror which was yet to overcome them was at that moment on the Atlantic, and hastening with fatal impetuosity towards these uncertain shores.

UNION

It was early in the month of September that intelligence reached France of the reception which the decree of the 15th of May had met with in Hayti. The tumult and horrid massacres which we have noticed were represented in their most affecting colors. Consequences more dreadful were still anticipated. The resolution of the whites never to allow the operation of the ill-fated decree was represented as immovable; and serious apprehensions were entertained for the loss of the colony.

The mercantile towns grew alarmed for the safety of their capitals, and petitions and remonstrances were poured in upon the National Assembly from every interested quarter for the repeal of that decree which they plainly foresaw must involve the colony in all the horrors of civil war, and increase those heaps of ashes which had already deformed its once beautiful plains.

The National Assembly, now on the eve of dissolution, listened with astonishment to the effects of a decree which, by acknowledging the rights of the mulattoes, it was expected would cover them with glory. The tide of popular opinion had begun to ebb; the members of the Assembly fluctuated in indecision; the friends of the planters seized each favorable moment to press their point, and actually procured a repeal of the decree at the same moment that it had become a medium of peace in Hayti.

At length the news reached these unhappy shores. The infatuated whites resolved to support the repeal, which would leave the mulattoes at their mercy. A sullen silence prevailed among the latter, interrupted at first by occasional murmurings and execrations, and finally exploding in a frenzy which produced the most diabolical excesses yet on record.

Rigaud's original motto was again revived, and each party seemed to aim at the extermination of the other. The mulattoes made a desperate attempt to capture Port au Prince, but the European troops lately arrived defeated them with considerable loss. They nevertheless set fire to the city, which lighted up a conflagration in which more than a third part of it was reduced to ashes.

Driven from Port au Prince, by the light of those flames which they had kindled, the mulattoes established themselves at La Croix Bouquets in considerable force, in which port they maintained themselves with more than equal address. At last, finding themselves and the revolted slaves engaged in a common cause, they contrived to unite their forces, and with this view drew to their body the swarms that resided in Cul de Sac. Augmented with these undisciplined myriads they risked a general engagement, in which two thousand blacks were left dead on the field; about fifty mulattoes were killed, and some taken prisoners. The loss of the whites was carefully concealed, but is supposed to have been equally as destructive.

The furious whites seized a mulatto chief whom they had taken prisoner, and, to their everlasting infamy, upon him they determined to wreak their vengeance. They placed him in a cart, driving large spiked nails through his feet into the boards on which they rested to prevent his escape, and to show their dexterity in torture. In this miserable condition he was conducted through the streets, and exposed to the insults of those who mocked his sufferings. He was then liberated from this partial crucifixion to suffer a new mode of torment. His bones were then broken in pieces, and finally he was cast alive into the fire, where he expired. So much for the whites.

The mulattoes, irritated to madness at the inhumanity with which one of their leaders had been treated, only awaited an opportunity to avenge his wrongs. Unfortunately, an opportunity soon occurred. In the neighborhood of Jerimie, M. Sejourne and his wife were seized. The lady was materially *enciente*. Her husband was first murdered before her eyes. They then ripped open her body, took out the infant and *gave it to the hogs;* after which they cut off her husband's head and entombed it in her bowels. "Such were the first displays of vengeance and retaliation, and such were the scenes that closed the year 1791."

"A law there is of ancient fame,
  By nature's self in every land implanted,
  Lex Talionis is its Latin name;
  But if an English term be wanted,
  Give our next neighbor but a pat,
  He'll give you back as good and tell you—*tit for tat!*

LETTER XII

Tragedy of the Revolution continued — Rigaud succeeded by
Toussaint — Toussaint duped by Le Clerc.

We omit, as unnecessary to the thread of this narrative,
the contentions between the French and English, in consequence of the British invasion, from 1792 to 1798; during which time Rigaud was succeeded by Toussaint
L'Ouverture, whose superior military genius had won for
him the appointment of Commander-in-Chief of the
native forces.

But there is yet another "lesson of the hour" to be
gleaned from the history of this marvellous revolution.
Treachery led to the fall of Toussaint.

On the 1st day of July, 1801, a Declaration of Independence was made by Toussaint, in the name of the
people.

The ancient proprietors of plantations, who in the
former insurrections had been compelled to quit the
island and seek an asylum in France, soon found in this
act of independence a confirmation of their former suspicions. They saw that all their valuable possessions must
be inevitably lost, and that forever, unless government
could be prevailed on to send an armed force to crush at
once a revolt which had become so formidable as to
assume independence.

The complicated interests of commerce were instantly alarmed and awakened to action; powerful parties were formed; a horde of venal writers started immediately into notice; a change was wrought in the
public sentiment as by the power of magic; and negro
emancipation was treated in just the same manner that
negro slavery had been treated before. Such was the fick-
leness of the French at that time, and such is the incon-
stancy of the human mind in ours.

Bonaparte, aiming himself at uncontrolled dominion, found it necessary to bribe all parties with gratifying promises to induce them to favor his views, and to enable him to introduce such changes in the form of government as he desired.

The transitory peace which had taken place in Europe produced at this time a band of desperate adventurers, who, destitute of employment, were ready for any enterprise that could afford them an opportunity to distinguish themselves. Accordingly an expedition of 26,000 men was fitted out, at the head of which was placed General Le Clerc;* and such was the confidence of its success, that he was accompanied by his wife, (sister to Napoleon,) and her younger brother Jerome Bonaparte.

But it was not to the fleet and army that Napoleon trusted exclusively for success. A number of plotting emissaries had been secretly dispatched to tamper with the unsuspecting blacks, to sow the seeds of discord between parties, and to shake their confidence in Toussaint. Even Toussaint's children had been prepared, by the deceitful caresses of the First Consul, to assist, by their representation of his conduct towards them, in the seduction of their father.

Le Clerc with his detachment of the French squadron, appeared off Cape François on the 5th day of January, 1802. General Christophe, who, during the absence of Toussaint, held the command, on perceiving the approach of the French fleet, immediately dispatched one of his officers to inform the commander of the squadron of Toussaint's absence, and to assure him he could not permit any troops to land until he had heard from the General-in-Chief. "That in case the direction of the expedition should persist in the disembarkation of his forces without permission, he should consider the white inhabitants in his district as hostages for his conduct, and, in consequence of any attack, the place attacked would be immediately consigned to the flames."

---

* Rainsford.

The inhabitants, trembling for their personal safety and the fall of the city, sent a deputation to assure Le Clerc that what had been threatened by Christophe would actually be realized should he persist in his attempt to land his forces.

Le Clerc, regardless of this destiny, and intent upon the gratification of his own ambition, proceeded to put on shore his troops, flattering himself with being able to gain the heights of the Cape before the blacks should have time to light up their threatened conflagration.

Christophe instantly perceived this movement, and, steady to his purpose, ordered his soldiers to defend themselves in their respective posts to the last extremity, and to sink if possible the ships of the assailants; but that when their own positions were no longer tenable, to remove whatever valuables could be preserved, reduce every thing besides to ashes, and retire.

Le Clerc did not reach the heights of the Cape until evening, and then only to behold the flames which Christophe had kindled, and which filled even the French soldiers with horror. They beheld with unavailing anguish the stately city in a blaze, the glare of which gilded the ceiling of heaven with a dismal light. Their expectation of a booty vanished in an instant, and the only reward which awaited them, they plainly perceived, was a heap of ashes or a bed of fire.

It was during these scenes of devastation on the shores that Toussaint was engaged in rendering the interior as formidable as possible; after the accomplishing of which he returned towards the ruins of the capital to discover if possible the real intentions of the French respecting the island, and to learn if any amicable proposition was to be made, which should secure to the inhabitants that freedom for which they had taken up arms.

In this moment of suspended rapine, Le Clerc resolved to try what effect a letter addressed personally to

Toussaint by Napoleon would have upon the black commander, who was yet unapprised of its existence, or of the arrival of his sons from France. A courier was immediately dispatched with the former, and with intelligence that the latter were with their mother on his plantation, called Ennerry.

The wife and children of Toussaint, ignorant of the part they were to play, entertained, as the author of their happiness, Coison, the preceptor of their children, who was at that moment plotting their destruction.

Toussaint, animated with the feelings of an affectionate parent, hastened, on the receipt of the letter and intelligence of the arrival of his children, to fold them in his warm embrace. He reached the plantation the ensuing night. When his arrival was announced, the mother shrieked, and instantly became insensible from a delirium of joy. The children ran to meet their father, and sunk without utterance into his open arms. When the first burst of joy was over, and the hero turned to caress him to whom he immediately owed the delight he had experienced, Coison began his attack. He recapitulated the letters of Bonaparte and Le Clerc; he invited him to accede to them, and represented the advantages resulting from his submission in such glowing colors as could hardly fail to awaken some suspicions. He perfidiously declared that the armament was not designed to abridge the liberty of the blacks, and concluded with observing that, unless the proposed conditions were immediately acceded to his orders were to return the children to the Cape.

Toussaint retired for a few moments from the presence of his wife and children, to weigh the import of their common supplication. His awakened reason instantly discovered the snare which had been laid to entrap him, and he therefore indignantly replied: "Take back my children, if it must be so; I will be faithful to my brethren and my God!"* then mounting his horse,

---

* Rainsford.

rode off to the camp, from which place he returned a formal answer to Le Clerc.

Unfortunately Le Clerc's bribery was not so ineffectual in other quarters. Many of Toussaint's generals were induced to listen to the promises of Le Clerc, and

"To sell for gold what gold could never buy."

Among these was an officer named La Plume, who by his treachery threw a large district into the hands of the French, and also revealed to them those plans of operation with which Toussaint had entrusted him.

Such an act on the part of La Plume, in whom Toussaint had placed unlimited confidence, could not but cause him to distrust those who remained attached to the common cause; and who, perceiving these suspicions, grew lax in the obedience which they owed to his commands.

On the 24th of February a severe battle took place between the French troops under General Rochambeau, and those under General Toussaint, consisting of 1,500 grenadiers, 1,200 other chosen soldiers, and 400 dragoons. The position of the blacks was extremely well chosen, being in a ravine fortified by nature and protected by works of art. Rochambeau, availing himself of his local knowledge of the country, which he had obtained from La Plume, entered the ravine with as much address as Toussaint could have manifested, avoided the obstacles which had been thrown in his way, and commenced an attack on the entrenchments of the blacks. Toussaint was prepared to receive him, and a desperate battle ensued, in which both skill and courage were alike conspicuous. The day was extremely bloody, and the field which victory hesitated to bestow on either party was covered with the bodies of the slain. Both parties at the close of the day retired from the scene of action to provide rather for their future safety than to renew a fierce contention for a mere point of honor.

Rochambeau hastened with the remains of his division to join the French troops in the western province, who were unable to withstand the force of the black General Maurepas. The troops thus collected were put in action, and the doubtful issue of battle was expected to decide their fortune. But Le Clerc had recourse to his usual manoeuvres, and Maurepas, seduced with the promise of retaining his rank under the auspices of Le Clerc, submitted to the French general without a struggle, and gave his posts into the enemy's hands.

Le Clerc, finding he could conquer the blacks much more readily by winning their confidence than by swords, redoubled his efforts in this direction. The number of his emissaries was increased; their powers were enlarged, and they were sent forth as the missionaries of seduction to induce the unsuspecting inhabitants to put on their chains. Success in proportion to his professions attended their exertions. Even Christophe was induced to believe that the late proclamations, in which Le Clerc promised liberty to all, were sincere. And, finally, Toussaint, willing to prevent the effusion of blood, gave way to the representations of Christophe, who immediately entered into correspondence with Le Clerc.

A truce was formed on the ground of an oblivion of the past, the freedom of the men in arms, and the preservation of his own rank, that of Toussaint and Dessalines, and all the officers in connection with them. This proposition was made by Christophe, and agreed to by Toussaint; but Dessalines, dreading such an unnatural compromise, submitted only under protest. The proposals, after some hesitation on the part of Le Clerc, were accepted.

Hostilities ceased on the 1st of May.

Not one month passed before Le Clerc seized Toussaint, his family, and about one hundred of his immediate associates, and placed them as prisoners on board the vessels then lying in the harbor. Many of the blacks were ordered to return to their labors under their ancient masters.

Toussaint, amazed at such an act of treachery and baseness, inquired the cause, but could obtain no other reply than that he must instantly depart. For himself he offered no excuse, declaring that he was ready to accompany his abductors in obedience to his orders; but as his wife was feeble and his children helpless, he begged earnestly that they might be permitted to remain. His expostulations were of course urged in vain.

Le Clerc, to rid the island for ever of a man whom he both feared and detested, prepared, soon after the capture of Toussaint, to send him to Europe, and with him a letter of accusation at once false, criminal, and malicious. A letter more dishonorable never crossed the Atlantic. Upon his arrival in France, Toussaint was immediately sent to prison in a remote province in the interior, and entirely secluded from the society of men.

Shut up in melancholy silence, in a dungeon horrid, damp, and cold, his suffering was not long. The Paris journals of April 27, 1803, say this—no more and no less: "Toussaint died in prison."

As to his wife and children, they remained in close custody at Brest for about two months after their only friend was torn from them. They were then removed to the same province in which Toussaint had been imprisoned, without knowing anything either of his proximity or his fate. In this place, reduced to distress, they continued neglected and forgotten, a sad spectacle of fallen greatness.

Such was the fate of Toussaint L'Ouverture, the *Washington,* but not *"the Napoleon,"* of Hayti.

LETTER XIII

The War Renewed — "Liberty or Death" —Expulsion of the French — The Aurora of Peace —Jean Jacques Dessalines, First Emperor of Hayti — Principal Events up to present date — Geffrard and Education — possible future.

> "This is the moral of all human tales:
> 'Tis but the same rehearsal of the past—
> First freedom, and then glory."
>
> —CHILDE HAROLD

The violent and perfidious measures to which Le Clerc had resorted produced an effect diametrically opposed to that which he intended. On the distant mountains, particularly toward the Spanish division, innumerable hosts of blacks had taken up their residence and assumed a species of lawless violence. They ridiculed every idea of a surrender to the Europeans, notwithstanding the compromise which had been made with Toussaint and Christophe. Even among those who had submitted, the sudden seizure of their brave leader and about one hundred of his enlightened associates, of whose fate they could receive no satisfactory account, but who were supposed to have been murdered by Le Clerc, produced a spirit of indignation which was poured forth in execrations portending an approaching storm.

Le Clerc, seated on his painful eminence, saw in a great measure the danger of his situation, and endeavored to counteract the impending evil. But death at this moment was lessening the number of his troops, and sickness disabling the survivors from performing the common duties of their stations.

Dessalines, whose talents and valor, recognized by his countrymen, had caused him to be appointed to act

as General-in-Chief, resolved not to dally with his faithless foes as Toussaint had done, but to bring this ferocious war to a speedy and decisive issue. Impressed with
this resolution, he drew a considerable force into the
plain of Cape François, with a design to attack the city.
Rochambeau, perceiving his movements, exerted himself
to strengthen the fortifications of the city, after which he
determined to risk a general engagement.

Both parties were as well prepared for the event
as circumstancs would admit. The attack was begun by
the French with the utmost resolution, and from the
violence of the onset the troops of Dessalines gave way
for a moment, and a considerable number fell prisoners
into the hands of the French. But the power and courage
of the blacks soon returned. The French were repulsed;
and as a body of them were marching to strengthen one
of the wings of their army, they were unexpectedly surrounded by the blacks, made prisoners of war, and driven
in triumph to their camp.

With these vicissitudes terminated the day. At night
the French general, to the disgrace of Europe, ordered
the black prisoners to be put to death. The order was
executed with circumstances of peculiar barbarity. Some
perished on the spot; others were mutilated in their
limbs, legs, and vital parts, and left in that horrible condition to disturb with their shrieks and groans the silence
of the night.

But Rochambeau had to deal with a very different
man from Toussaint—a man whose motto was, *"Never
to retaliate;"* for under cover of the same inauspicious
night Dessalines deliberately selected the officers from
among his prisoners, then added a number of privates,
and gibbeted them all together in a place most exposed
to the French army.

Nor did the revenge of the black soldiers terminate
even here. Burning with indignation against the men
whose conduct had stimulated them to such inhuman

deeds, they rushed down upon the French the ensuing morning, destroyed the camp, made a terrible slaughter, and compelled the flying fugitives to take refuge under the walls of Cape François. From this period the French were unable to face their opponents in the open field, and the victorious Dessalines immediately took steps to crush them in the city.

To add to the calamities of the French commander, the war between England and France was again renewed during this period of distress. Unfortunately, however, he remained uninstructed by past experience, and his cruelty seemed to increase with the desperation of his circumstances. Pent up in the city, from which his forces durst not venture in a body, he contrived to detach small parties with bloodhounds to hunt down a few straggling negroes, who wandered through the woods unconscious of the impending danger. These when taken were seized with brutal triumph, and thrown to the dogs to be devoured alive.

Amid scenes and horrors as infamous as these, Le Clerc was summoned by the fever to appear before a higher tribunal to give an account of his deeds of darkness. He died on the 1st of November, after having been driven from Tortuga, his previous place of abode. Madame Le Clerc was present at the awful scene; then, departing with the body for Europe, bade a final farewell to a region which had promised her happiness, but paid her with anguish and mortification.

It was in the month of July that an English squadron, not fully apprised of the condition of the French army, made its appearance off the cape. This circumstance completely overwhelmed the besieged commander, who, while the blacks were fiercely crowding upon him, was perfectly conscious of his vulnerable condition as exposed to the British. He therefore opened a communication with the latter to learn what terms of capitulation he had to expect in case a proposition of that kind should be made. The terms required by the British being dreadfully severe, Rochambeau lost no time in strengthening the works towards the sea as well as towards the land, having every thing to fear from both quarters.

Meanwhile the victorious blacks continued to pour in reinforcements upon the plains of the cape. A powerful body now descended upon the French, and, having passed the outer lines and several blockhouses, prepared to storm the city in thirty-six hours.

Rochambeau, from a persuasion that all would be put to the sword, proceeded before it was too late to offer articles of capitulation, which, to the honor of Dessalines, by forgoing the desire of revenge, were accepted, granting the French ten days to evacuate the city—"an instance of forbearance and magnanimity," says Rainsford, "of which there are not many examples in ancient or modern history."

The articlesof capitulation which Rochambeau had entered into were communicated by Dessalines to the British commodore. The latter, therefore, awaited the expiration of the appointed time to mark the important event. When the time had elapsed, Commodore Loring, perceiving no movement of the French towards evacuation, sent a letter to General Dessalines to inquire if any alteration had taken place subsequent to his last communication, and if not, to request him to send some pilots on board to conduct his squadron into the harbor to take possession of the French shipping. To this letter he received the following characteristic reply:—

"LIBERTY or DEATH!

"Head-Quarters, *Nov.* 27, 1803.
"The Commander-in-Chief of the Native Army to Commodore Loring, etc., etc.:

"S i r :—I acknowledge the receipt of your letter and you

may be assured that my disposition toward you and against General Rochambeau is invariable.

"I shall take possession of the cape to-morrow morning at the head of my army. It is a matter of great regret to me that I cannot send you the pilots which you require. I presume that you will have no occasion for them, as I shall compel the French vessels to quit the road, and you will do with them what you shall think proper.

"I have the honor to be, etc., etc.

"DESSALINES."

Scarcely had Commodore Loring entered the harbor on the morning of the 30th, before he was met by an officer of the French troops then going in quest of the English to request them to take possession of the ships in the name of His Britannic Majesty. This, he observed, was the only method left by which they could be saved from inevitable destruction, as the black general was at that moment preparing to fire upon them with red-hot shot, and the wind, blowing directly into the mouth of the harbor, prevented their departure.

The whole of the French troops and shipping, including seventeen merchant vessels and about 8,000 soldiers and seamen, thus falling into the hands of the British, were conveyed to England, arriving at Portsmouth on the 3d of February, 1804, from whence the troops were taken into the interior and paroled as prisoners of war.

Thus ended his visionary expedition through which Napoleon and Le Clerc flattered themselves and the country that the inhabitants of Hayti were to be again reduced to slavery; and thus, by the unrelenting determination of Dessalines, were the fearful thunderbolts of war made to recoil on the heads of those who hurled them.

THE AURORA OF PEACE

The "Aurora of Peace" which Dessalines and his colleagues had predicted, was now ushered in. On the 14th of May following Dessalines departed from the cape, determined, like his unfortunate predecessor Toussaint, to make a tour through the island, to note the manners which prevailed, and to observe how far the regulations he had already introduced were enforced, and what beneficial effects had resulted from their adoption.

During this journey the people, animated by the presence of their victorious chief, resolved to exalt him to the dignity of emperor. Whether any intrigue had been used on this occasion by Dessalines, or that the offer was a pure emanation of gratitude originating with the people, it is impossible to say. This much, however, is certain, that the proposal was accepted without any reluctance, and in due time he was enthroned as *Jean Jacques Dessalines, the first emperor of Hayti.* This was at Port au Prince, on the 8th of October.

After the imposing ceremonies which necessarily attended the imperial coronation, the people, not forgetful of Him who had guided them through this arduous struggle in defence of those rights with which He had originally endowed them, marched to the church, where a Te Deum was sung to commemorate the important transactions of this memorable day. From this place of solemnity the whole procession returned in the order in which they came to the government house; after which a grand illumination took place in all parts of the city, amid the roaring of cannon and every demonstration of joy that both language and action could possibly express.

In tracing the narrative of this remarkable revolution, we have purposely omitted the invasion of the British from 1793 to 1798. Suffice it to say, that after a profuse waste of blood and treasure during five years, Great Britain was constrained to withdraw the remnant of her troops, acknowledge the independence of the island as a neutral power, and relinquish forever all pretensions to Hayti.

Such, then, is a brief outline of the principal features in the history of this new-born empire, as recorded by Edwards, Rainsford, and Coke, and as given me from the lips of veterans yet upon the soil. The principal changes since are briefly these:

The reign of the emperor Dessalines was short and turbulent and his designs against the mulattoes cost him his life. After the death of Dessalines, (in 1807,) General Christophe was made chief magistrate, and in 1811 he crowned himself King Henri I. Meanwhile the mulattoes having cause to distrust him also, elected General Petion, a companion of Rigaud, to preside in the south-west, which he did with great leniency and to the entire satisfaction of his constituents, by many of whom he is still affectionately remembered. He died in 1818. Christophe shot himself in 1820. In 1822, Boyer, who had been elected President, united the whole island under his government.

And this brings the chain of events up to those mentioned in our review of the history of the Spanish part of the island, to which the reader can refer for a statement of the principal changes from that time to the present.

Under President Geffrard the country is highly prosperous, such confidence being placed in the government that its paper currency is preferred by the people to silver coin.

Under Protestant influences, also, several large schools, in which hundreds of young girls and boys are being educated, promise in due time to present to the world a virtuous female offspring of these heroic revolutionists, adorned by all the graces attending the use of both the French and English languages, and a body of youths skilled at once in commerce, and in the sciences of government, the sword, the anvil, and the plow.

The president desires the immigration hither of young men and ladies who are capable of teaching French, "and also to undertake," he says, "the courses of our lyceums. In this case they would find employment immediately."

It is difficult to believe these fields of natural beauty, embellished with all the decorations of art, have at any time presented to earth and heaven such spectacles of horror as to cause even Europe, accustomed as it is to blood and fire, to stand aghast, and which will serve Americans as a finger-board of terror so long as slavery there exists. The torch of conflagration and the sword of destruction have marched in fearful union through the land, and covered the hills and plains with desolation. Tyranny, scorn, and retaliating vengeance have displayed their utmost rage, and in the end have given birth to an empire which has not only hurled its thunderbolts on its assailants, but at this moment bids defiance to the world.

In the days of imperial Rome it was the custom of Cicero and his haughty contemporaries to sneer at the wretchedness and barbarity of the Britons, just as Americans speak of Haytiens to-day; yet when we reflect how analogous the history of the seven-hilled city and that of the United States promises to be, that Hayti may yet become the counterpart of England, head-quarters of a colored American nationality, and supreme mistress of the Caribbean sea, she can well afford to leave

"Things of the future to fate."

LETTER XIV

Grand Turk's and Caicos Islands

An Island of Salt — Sir Edward Jordan, of Jamaica — Honor
to the British Queen — A Story in Parenthesis — The Poetry
of Sailing.

> "Had ancient poets known this little spot—
> Poets who formed rich Edens in their thought—
> Arcadia's vales, Calypso's verdant bowers,
> Hesperia's groves, and Tempe's gayest flowers,
> Had ne'er appeared so beautiful and fair
> As these gay rocks and emerald islands are."

It is usually no more to "dangle round" this sea than it
is to cross Lake Erie. On this particular occasion, however, I very willingly reached these shores, for the little
schooner Enterprise in which we had ventured was not
much larger than a good-sized yawl—certainly not over
six tons burthen. The waves inundated us at pleasure,
wetting even the letters in my breast coat-pocket, filling
our faces at times with its slashing foam, and drenching
us thoroughly to the inmost thread. But our schooner
skimmed along like a seagull, and within thirty-two hours
we were once again on land, dry enough for all practical
purposes. Nice little schooner—the waves might as well
have undertaken to drown a fish!

There is not a natural hill on all Turk's Island. The
shores are but a few feet above the level of the sea, and
the interior is scooped out like a basin. This basin
is artifically subdivided into innumerable troughs or
ponds, into which water is admitted by canals from the
sea, whence it evaporates leaving beds of salt. This salt
is then raked into hills, so that as you approach these

shores you have the extraordinary sight of an island studded with salt-hills.

The slight elevation of the land also permits the wind to pass uninterruptedly over its limestone surface, which accounts for the even temperature and perfect health of the island. The thermometer fell to-day from 86° to 77° Fahrenheit, which is the hottest and the coldest they have had it this summer. But, as you will readily perceive, the absence of all barriers to the winds subjects the colony to the terrific ravages of every ocean storm that chooses to sweep this way. At this very moment the large and substantial mansion in which I am writing trembles like an aspen-leaf, and I am fearful that the few cocoa-nut trees and flower plants bending before the storm on every side will be speedily swept away. Heaven spare the verdure!—the people can look out for themselves. Generally speaking, the winds are soft as a sigh. The gale ebbs to a gentle zephyr; the cloud passes on to Mobile, or wherever else it is bound, leaving these islands gayer for its shower; the huge West Indian sun, apparently magnified to six times its usual diameter, sinks into the crimsoned sea; the heavenly twilight comes on once more, and earth, sea, and sky are all once again tranquilly imparadised. The effect of these transitions on the mind is imperative. The most commonplace, matter-of-fact personage you have in America can not spend a summer around these islands and amid these scenes without having transitory poetic visions flash through his inmost being. But do not think I intend to dwell any further on these Elysian things. If you have a correspondent capable of describing them, send him along. A keen sense of my inability to do so constrains me to desist as from an attempt to comprehend the Infinite.

According to the theory of certain American statesmen, Turk's Island properly belongs to Hayti; at least, it is on the borders of the Haytien sea, and and is as much beholden to Hayti for its support as Cuba is to the

United States. As luck has it, however, Turk's Island really belongs to the British, and Cuba, it would seem.

"By some o'er hasty angel was misplaced."

These, then, are a group of the celebrated British West Indies, and form a part of the governmental jurisdiction of Jamaica. It is with rare pleasure that I mention the latter fact, (since "next to being great one's self it is desirable to have a true relish for greatness,") for it gives me an opportunity to inform you that the order of knighthood has recently been conferred by Her Britannic Majesty on Sir Edward Jordan, Mayor of the city of Kingston and Prime Minister of Jamaica—a degree of dignity never before attained by a colored man, as I believe, since the British government began. The day of the Anglo-African in America has not yet clearly dawned, but it is dawning. A great many of the officers here, too, are colored. How strange it seems to stand before a large, fine-looking black or colored man, entitled Sir, Honorable, Esquire, and the like! To save me, I cannot realize it, although I see, hear, and shake hands with them every day.

But the grand source of interest to you and to me is, of course, the slaves manumitted by the magnanimity of the British government some twenty-six years agone. It is strangely interesting to hear them tell of parties making their escape to Hayti by sail-boats previous to the act of emancipation, sometimes sailing swift and direct, and at others dodging under the lee of the Caicos reefs until pursuit had been suspended, reminding one much of our Canadian friends. The history of the escape of slaves in our day is as full of heroism as any history in the world.

The neatness and cleanly appearance of the masses are actually surprising. I say it with all due respect, but, take them all in all, the colored people really present a better appearance than the whites. The latter, however, for reasons which you will already have anticipated, are of course more wealthy and intelligent—for which reason, also, they have heretofore been entirely at the head of political affairs. It is only recently that the blacks, who are in the majority, began to tread on their political heels. Some of the whites do not like to see this, but the easiest way for them is to allow themselves to be peacefully absorbed by the colored race in these regions, for their destiny is sealed.

The Caicos Islands, like most of the Bahamas, are but a series of coral reefs, more extensive in territory and less sterile than this portion of the colony; but their principal products are about the same—salt and shipwrecks. They are at once "the residence and the empire of danger." An American captain is now here selling the wreck of a cargo lately shipped from Boston to New Orleans—(Captain Elliot, ship Nauset, total wreck on North Caicos reef, July 7, 1860.) The population of the group inclusive is about five thousand, principally colored, who are remarkably industrious, if one is to judge from the rapidity with which they load a vessel with salt; and the essentially limited resources of the island would seem to admit of their being equally virtuous. Churches abound, and schooling may be had at the rate of three cents per week. Every thing is due to the English missionary societies for the healthy tone of morality and religion which prevails in these islands, and I must say, as I believe, chiefly to the Baptists.

But the great characteristic and most amusing peculiarity of these people is their inordinate attachment to the British crown. A captain of a schooner on the coast (black, but thoroughly British) one day overheard some reckless fellow speak disrespectfully of Queen Victoria. About every thing he thought of or said during the rest of the voyage was, "He insult my Queen," repeating "He insult my Queen" over and over again. They seem to regard Queen Victoria with about the same reverence that the Spanish Catholics bestow upon the Virgin Mary. Nor do I blame them for this, since, if England were crippled to-day, it would be difficult to say what would become of the world's humanity. It would be like extinguishing the sun!

Every thing is salty. You stand a chance to get some Boston ice here, which is a *rara avis* in this direction; but before you can get it congealed into cream you are bound to get salt into it, it would seem. A nice saloon, a good hotel, three churches, (English, Wesleyan, and Baptist,) and a first class Masonic lodge—at the head of which is a colored Esquire—together with its excessive salt propensities, are about the best things that can be said for Grand Turk's Island. Stay! I forget the "Royal Standard," a weekly journal, to the editor of which I am under obligations, and from which I clip the following

NOTICE

On the first of August, the "Friendly Society" and the "Benevolent Union Society" of Salt Cay will march in procession from the Society Hall, at 11 o'clock A.M., to the Baptist chapel, where a sermon will be preached by the Rev. W. K. Rycoft on the occasion. By order, etc.,

JOHN L. WILLIAMS.

So much for the land of salt, and a farewell to its happy people, the most that can be said of whom is that they worship Queen Victoria.

(Let me tell you a story. In passing around these islands, we are one day with the Spanish, next day with the English, and the third with the French. It is sometimes diverting. I was sitting one warm afteroon before the door of a countryhouse, having a large green sward-yard sloping away to the road. The house was full of children, some of whom were, or pretended to be, studying their books. Well, suddenly there came pouring down a splendid summer shower, when, without a word, half a dozen of these little rogues, of both sexes, dropped their books, stripped off to the skin, and away they went sailing around the yard like so many water nymphs! In five minutes more they were all dressed, sitting down with their books, and looking as demure as if nothing had happened. "So there hadn't," except that one plump little girl *fell heels over head!* That is one way of taking a shower bath I never thought of.)

By the way, an American captain was this day looking at a number of hands, male and female, engaged in loading a vessel with salt. The women were employed holding the sacks, and tying them when filled.

"That's a smart gal," said the Yankee captain, pointing to an ebon Venus who was singing, dancing, and tossing the sacks around as merrily as your city girls ever "pawed" the piano.

A sleek-faced gentleman turned up his eyes at us, and inquired: "You lub dis gal, Cap'en?"

"Thunder, no!" said the astonished American; "I don't love anybody!" Which remark, I guess, was not very far from the truth.

The vessel which I am now on board of is a full-rigged, finely-finished English brig. Her sails are all set, the wind blows fresh, and she cuts the water like a sword-fish. The captain cleared $1,400 on his trip out, with a cargo of lumber from the States. How much will our friend Wm. Whipper* make in a year running his craft up a Canadian creek? The tenacity with which our leading colored men embrace that short-sighted policy which teaches them to confine their enterprises to certain proscribed, prejudice-cursed districts, is not only extraordinary—it is marvellous.

The heavenly night comes on. The clouds in the sky look like ships on fire. The rising moon trembles upon the silver-sheeted waves in the east, while the receding sun burnishes the west, tinging the waters even to our

---

* See introduction.

very spray. And thus, in this sea of glory, do we skim along. *This* is the "poetry of sailing."

> "Thou glorious, shining, billowy sea,
> With ecstasy I gaze on thee!
> And as I gaze, thy billowy roll
> Wakes the deep feelings of my soul."

LETTER XV

British Honduras

The Island of Ruatan — The Sailor's Love Story — The
Sovereignty of the Bay Islands — English vs. American View
of Central American Affairs.

*Off Ruatan the New "Gibralter," Flower of the
Bay Islands, and "Key to Spanish America."*

It certainly takes the impatience out of one to travel very
much on a sail vessel. The dead certainty of your getting
becalmed annihilates even contrary anticipation. But instead of murmuring at the irksome roll of this spell-
bound ship, which flaps its sails as vainly as a bird with
cropped wings, I, with genuine Spartan philosophy, will
make the most of it by going visiting, that is, from the
cabin to the forecastle. Here I take a seat beside an
American; (for, my dear H., nobody ever knows what
true friendship is until they have been shipwrecked, nor
does any one conceive how mutual are the sympathies of
persons coming from the same country, however remote
their positions may have been, until they have met away
from home, and been surrounded by foreign influences.
Strange as it may seem, I have not met a colored American out this way but who actually celebrates the Fourth
of July.)

Instead of complaining of this ghastly calm, as I
was about to say, I take a seat beside my friend Mr.
Johnson, formerly of Plymouth, Massachusetts, from
whom I learned the following important story, albeit, a
love story. Important because it shows the correctness of

157

that theory which assumes this,—the infusion of Northern blood as one of the means by which the more sluggish race of the tropics is to be quickened and given energy, and also how these seductive southern zones induce persons to sacrifice kindred, friends, and home, in order to live and die under their soothing influences.

The story is this: Some years ago he had sailed from Boston to Balize with a cargo of ice; was taken sick, and the captain of his vessel, having made all possible arrangements for his comfort, left him in the hospital to recover. He did so, and was just on the eve of going over to Jamaica to get on board a vessel in which to return home, when up stepped an elderly man, who accosted him in English and also in Yankee, to wit: "Guess you are from the States?" to which Mr. Johnson replied, of course, "You, too, I suppose?" The fact is, if you could not tell an American away from home by his looks, his salutatory phrases are as certain as an oddfellow's password.

So Mr. Dickinson, the elderly gentleman, was from the States also, and nothing would do but Mr. Johnson must accompany him to his home in Ruatan, there to spend a few weeks for old acquaintance' sake, and meanwhile strengthen his health. He went; but Mr. Johnson coming from the States had never seen so lovely an island, and certainly none so prolific as Ruatan. He found oranges selling for one dollar per barrel, and cocoa-nuts at a cent apiece; and that after being rowed a distance of six miles. He found also that good milch cows could be bought for six dollars each; and that upon one of the neighboring islands wild cattle were to be had for the sport of catching. On Utille, another island, also, almost in sight of Ruatan, is a settlement of whites, which, though small, is in a very flourishing condition; both being tributary to Ruatan. Altogether, he liked the appearance of things exceedingly.

Mr. Johnson not being one of your lazy visitors, soon began to make himself useful by assisting his friend Mr. Dickinson in whatever he might have to do; and so one day, with pants rolled up to his knees, he went over to a neighbor's to borrow some bags. This neighbor had a pretty niece who lived in Nicaragua, which is just over the way, and who was now on a visit to her uncle.

It was near dusk; his neighbor was not at home; but, with that careless indifference which travellers in the tropics will appreciate, he walked into the shanty, slightly nodded to some one he saw sitting in the corner, and immediately stretched himself out in a hammock.

The timid girl, less frightened at this rude freedom than at the bushy whiskers of the Northerner, answered his inquiries as to when her uncle would be in, curtsied, and left the room; but in doing so she discovered about the trimmest ancle and the neatest pair of stockings Mr. Johnson had ever beheld. It fixed him. He could not sleep after that without dreaming of the pretty feet, and, of course, pretty owner.

Mr. Johnson found business with his neighbor very often. The divinity went over home; Mr. Johnson had business over there also; and with genuine American grit obtained the old man's consent, and actually returned with his daughter.

Soon after this Mr. Johnson received from the States the mournful intelligence of his father's death, and, like a dutiful son, immediately sailed for Plymouth to see his mother and sisters. His brother, equally anxious with his mother and friends to have him stop at home, offered him a situation as clerk in a lawyer's office. But, alas! those pretty feet! They had caused him to sacrifice his home; and although shipwrecked in the attempt, he is now back in Ruatan, with no expectation of ever meeting his Plymouth friends again during life. "I told them," he said, "she was not quite so white as some of them, but she's a darn sight better-hearted;" which is very probably a fact. Mr. Johnson affirmed, also, that he could not be induced to leave Ruatan for the income of the most princely merchant in Boston; but I make allowance for a man who has a young wife with pretty feet.

Ruatan, as you are aware, is the principal one of the celebrated Bay Islands, the sovereignty of which has been so long in dispute. Nor can I settle the question as to whether the British claim is just or not; I can only give it to you as I get it.

In the first place you must know there is what may be called *two Honduras*. That is, the State of Honduras, and these Bay Islands with a portion of the Musquito coast, constituting British Honduras, of which Balize is the capital. This will relieve a great many blunders people have perpetually fallen into.

When or by whom Ruatan was originally settled is now unknown. It was discovered by the Spaniards, and was afterwards occupied as a military post, but subsequently abandoned. Soon after the Emancipation Act took effect in Jamaica and the other British isles, a number of these emancipated slaves settled here, and the settlement is now multiplied to the number of about three thousand.

It becoming necessary for them to have a government, they sent to Jamaica for a magistrate to act as governor, voting him a salary of three thousand dollars, and, being British subjects, of course looked to Great Britain for protection. And so Great Britain claims the right to protect them; and she does protect them.

It was off this island that the pirate Walker* rendezvoused the present summer; and from what I have said respecting the immigration hither of a few white Americans, you will probably suppose there might be some advantage taken of these islanders; but do not think it. Mr. William Walker's recent experience at Truxillo will probably induce him to respect Ruatan.

---

* William Walker, American filibuster. Died before a Honduran firing squad in 1860.

Nevertheless, Ruatan is measurably affected, of course, by the prosperity of the main land, and if the future administration of the United States government is to be as weak and vacillating as the past has been, it is difficult to say what is to be the end of these invasions.

At present there is but little communication between this excellent island and the United States. Thanks to your unjust policy, (wide-spread infamy,) the natives can not be induced to look towards America, and so can not see the difference between the Northern and Southern States. This feeling has been heightened recently by the fact that a merchant, who dealt in fruits with certain parties in New Orleans, went over there on business. He was also a British magistrate, and took with him the necessary papers to certify that fact. Hardly had he reached the shore before he was arrested and taken to prison; and when he supposed to estop their procedure by showing that he was a British magistrate, the New Orleans constable replied: "If Queen Victoria were to come over here, and she were black, I'd put her in jail!"

I am asked to point out, as I go along, what could be done whereby persons could gain a competence? Any thing in the shape of work will gain a competence,—the trouble being, in all these countries, that a living is too easily gained. But fruits are the principal export. Could a vessel be run between this and Baltimore, or any other respectable port of the United States, it would pay beyond a peradventure. It would also furnish the means of getting here safe the fruits from wasting, for want of occasional vessels, and also supply news; which is an inconceivable desideratum.

Land is offered at a shilling an acre; import duty is but two per cent, and exports free; which, considering the English language prevails, give it a decided advantage as a place of settlement.

Ruatan is but thirty miles from Truxillo, Honduras, and one hundred and twenty from Balize; and these are the only ways of getting here from New York, at a cost of sixty dollars. For the want of such a vessel as I have intimated, crops of oranges and limes are frequently swept into the sea. The Pine-apples are large and of a superior quality. Walk out into the grounds early in the morning, take a Machette and strike one open, and nothing can give you an idea of their flavor except to imagine you are sipping the nectar of the gods.

In the interior of the island are cocoa-nut groves, and other marks of improvement, such as an old fortress hid away from the sea, which clearly prove the island to have been anciently inhabited; but, like many other interesting objects which the historian fails to comprehend, by whom, or when, is left entirely to the conception of the poets.

> "Gone are all the barons bold;
> Gone are all the knights and squires;
> Gone the abbot, stern and cold,
> And the brotherhood of friars."

ENGLISH *vs.* AMERICAN VIEW OF CENTRAL AMERICAN AFFAIRS

It is but fair to say the Hon. E. G. Squier* shows very clearly the forced nature of the English claims, and that Ruatan rightly belongs to Honduras. But then I should think Mr. Squier, or any other American, would blush to talk about British *proclivities to piracy.*

The following are the views of Mr. Trollope (English) on the most important of Central American affairs,†

---

*Squier was an American journalist and archaeologist, chargé d'affaires to the Central American republics in 1849-50. He is the author of several works on the area, including *Travels in Central America. . . .* (2 vols., New York: D. Appleton & Co., 1853.) A revised one-volume edition was published by Harper and Brothers, 1860. Under the pseudonym of Samuel A. Bard Squier also wrote *Waikna; or Adventures on the Mosquito Shore* (New York: Harper and Brothers, 1855). H. H. B.

†Anthony Trollope's *West Indies and Spanish Main.* Harper and Brothers, 1860.

who probably also intends by them to give Mr. S. a rap on the knuckles.

"As I have before stated, there was, some few years since, a considerable passenger traffic through Central American by the route of the lake of Nicaragua. This of course was in the hands of the Americans, and the passengers were chiefly those going and coming between the Eastern States and California. They came down to Greytown at the mouth of the San Juan river, in steamers from New York, and, I believe, from various American ports, went up the San Juan river in other steamers, with flat bottoms, prepared for those waters, across the lake in the same way, and then by a good road over the intervening neck of land between the lake and the Pacific.

"Of course the Panama Railway has done much to interfere with this. In the first place, a rival route has thus been opened; though I doubt whether it would be a quicker route from New York to California if the way by the lake were well organized. And then, the company possessing the line of steamers running to Aspinwall from New York has been able to buy off the line which would otherwise run to Greytown.

"But this rivalship has not been the main cause of the total stoppage of the Nicaraguan route. The filibusters came into that land and destroyed every thing. They dropped down from California, or Realego, Leon, Managua, and all the western coast of Nicaragua. Then others came from the South-eastern States, from Mobile, and New Orleans, and swarmed up the river San Juan, devouring every thing before them.

"There can be no doubt that Walker's idea, in his attempt to possess himself of this country, was, that he should become master of the passage across the Isthmus. He saw, as so many others have seen, the importance of the locality in this point of view; and he probably felt that if he could make himself lord of the soil, by his own exertions and on his own bottom, his mother country, the United States, would not be slow to recognize him. 'I' he would have said, 'have procured for you the ownership of the road which is so desirable for you. Pay me by making me your lieutenant here, and protecting me in that position.'

"The idea was not badly planned, but it was of course radically unjust. It was a contemplated filching of the road. And Walker found, as all men do find, that he could not get good tools to do bad work. He tried the job with a very rough lot of tools; and now, though he has done much harm to others, he has done very little good to himself. I do not think we shall hear much more of him.

"And among the worst injuries which he has done in this disturbance of the lake traffic. This route has been altogether abandoned. There, in the San Juan river, is to be seen one old steamer, with its bottom upwards, a relic of the filibusters and their destruction.

"All along the banks tales are told of their injustice and sufferings. How recklessly they robbed on their journey up the country, and how they returned to Greytown—those who did return whose bones are not whitening the lake shores—wounded, maimed, and miserable.

"Along the route traders were beginning to establish themselves; men prepared to provide the travellers with food and drink, and the boats with fuel for their steam. An end for the present has been put to all this. The weak governments of the country have been able to afford no protection to these men, and, placed as they were beyond the protection of England or the United States, they have been completely open to attack. The filibusers for a while have destroyed the transit through Nicaragua; and it is hardly matter of surprise that the president of that land, the neighboring republic, should catch at any scheme which proposes to give them back this advantage, especially when promise is made of the additional advantage of effectual protection.

"To us Englishmen it is a matter of indifference in whose hands the transit may be, so long as it is free and open to the world; so long as a difference of nationality creates no difference in the fares charged, or in the facilities afforded. For our own purposes I have no doubt the Panama line is the best, and will be the route we shall use. But we should be delighted to see a second line opened. If Mr. Squier can accomplish his line through Honduras we shall give him great honor, and acknowledge that he has done the world a service. Meantime we shall be very happy to see the lake transit reestablished."

There is no hope for the Central American States except by intervention on the part of some government capable of protecting them.

LETTER XVI

Conclusive Summary

Concise Description of the Spanish Main — Dominicana Reviewed — The magnificent Bay of Samana — Conclusive Summary.

Thus have I endeavored to seize on whatever might seem to be of importance, and at the same time interesting to such of your readers as desired to have some more general information respecting tropical America.

I am aware that I have not analyzed the soil, nor (so long as it produced well) have I cared whether it was "composed of the *débris* of these limestones and lava mountains," or "tempered by the decaying vegetation of the centuries past." Nor have I entered into any essay to show how the lofty sierras of Honduras differed from those of Nicaragua, or those of the islands from the Spanish Main. It would be easy to give you a chapter stating that "the summits of some of them are of hard sandstone or granite; some are covered with layers of mould of different colors and density, sometimes mixed with stones of different degrees of hardness, and more or less calcinable; and some of them of various vitrifiable substances." But I take it that the way to make a thing useful is also to have it agreeable. Who reads, for example, Mr. Wells'* well-written but ponderous "Travels and Explorations in Honduras"?

Central America, by common assent, not only realizes

---

* Harris is probably referring to William Vincent Wells' *Explorations and Adventures in Honduras, Comprising Sketches of Travel.* . . . New York: Harper and Brothers, 1857. H. H. B.

in its geographical position the ancient idea of the centre of the world, but is in its physical aspect and configuration of surface an epitome of all the countries and of all climes. "High mountain ranges, isolated peaks, elevated table lands, and broad and fertile plains, are here grouped together, relieved by beautiful lakes and majestic rivers; the whole teeming with animal and vegetable life, and possessing every variety of climate from torrid heat to the cool and bracing temperature of eternal spring."

On the Atlantic slope rain falls in greater or less abundance for the entire year; vegetation is rank, and the climate damp and proportionately insalubrious, while the Pacific slope and the elevated regions of the interior are comparatively dry and healthy.

With this variety of "physical circumstances," also, the people differ, and have always differed, in a direct and corresponding ratio; the inhabitants of the cool and healthy regions having at the time of the discovery systematized forms of government and worship, while the hotter and less salubrious coasts were occupied by a distinct family of men unfixed in their abodes, having no social enjoyments, and living on the natural fruits of the earth. In Central America, therefore, Dr. Smith's celebrated essay on "Civilization—its Independence of Physical Circumstance," receives a striking illustration, the damp Musquito coasts having propagated only a rude tribe of men; while San Salvador, for example, sustains a population highly civilized, and equal in number to New England.

But I have dwelt at most length on the island of Hayti, because it is a source of greatest interest to us, and

---

* Dr. James McCune Smith, perhaps one of the most influential black leaders of the period. Educated in the African Free Schools of New York and the University of Glasgow, Dr. Smith made his living by practicing medicine, but was a capable writer and an activist in improving conditions for the Negro. The article here mentioned appeared in the *Anglo-African Magazine*, January, 1859. H. H. B.

because there is perhaps no country the intrinsic value of which is so little known; and while I can see no objection but every thing to encourage by governmental influence the establishment of a colony in some parts of the Central American States, neither do I know why it might not be established in the Spanish territory of Hayti. I have given another gentleman's views, which are worth more than my own, as to the vast population the country is capable of sustaining, and have shown that especially from Porto Cabello west, to the Bay of Samana east, no finer province could certainly be desired. That noble bay, as I am informed, has been surveyed heretofore by a corps of American engineers, who pronounced it the choicest point for a naval station on the Caribbean coasts. It is also assumed, from the rapid increase of the coral reefs in the Bahama channels, that this in time will furnish the only safe channel for California steamers, and even for larger vessels bound from the Northern States to New Orleans. I have nothing to do with that, further than to state it as I have it. The insurance companies will however appreciate this assumption, if we are to judge from the number of wrecks which have recently occurred between the Caicos and Florida reefs.

Surrounding the bay of Samana are beds of coal as if on purpose to supply such steamers; but they now lie unworked, useless, and almost unknown. Into this bay empties the Yuna river, which takes its rise far back in the northern and middle range of mountains, and, fed by innumerable tributaries, winds its course towards this magnificent harbor through the widest portion of the Royal plains.

"In briefly describing the principal bays of Dominicana," says Mr. Courtney, "the first of importance is the far-famed and magnificent bay of Samana, at the northeastern end of the island, at the mouth of the Yuna river. It is about fifty miles from east to west, and varying in width from fifteen to twenty miles, and of a great depth. The entrance to it is at the east end, and is about a mile wide, as beyond that is shoal water, to the south side some little islands and bars appearing above the surface. An old fort, erected long since on the high bluff on the north side, a few miles above the mouth and before it widens out, commands its entrance. The hills and mountains on either side of the bay rise back from it to a great height, their sides being covered with beautiful slopes, plateaus, and benches. The coasts are here and there indented with minor bays and inlets, the most important of which is at the town of Samana, about twenty-five miles up the bay on the north side. It is a land-locked harbor and very deep, as are all the inlets. The view of the bay from either side across to the opposite shores, covered as it is with swarms of ducks and swans and other water fowl; and the coasts and hills and mountains covered with flowers and verdure and fruit, is truly beautiful and sublime, equalling, if not surpassing, in beauty and magnificence, the Bay of Naples, and is obviously the key to the Gulf of Mexico.

"Here all the navies of the world could lie at anchor in safety."

It would be useless for me to give a minute description of each particular bay in each particular State, thus swelling these pages into the usual ponderous three-dollar volumes which nobody buys, and so none read. I am aware that the Bay of Fonseca, and others on the Spanish Main, are equally deserving, if necessary, to be described. Mr. Wells has shown this, and also that the interior districts of Honduras are as rich in silver and gold as any region of which California can boast. I understand, however, that parties have since been formed on the strength of Mr. Wells' report, and thoroughly equipped for mining operations. But as I am informed, they were not allowed to enter the interior in consequence of those filibustering propensities which all white Americans are supposed to possess.

A party organized to work the mines on a small scale in Dominicana has lately sailed for the island. They will not be interrupted by the present government, but the durability of that government is, I am sorry to say, a question which may be agitated, and even settled, *before I finish writing this book.*

And now I have struck the key note of all I have to say. The most beautiful countries in the world are the most lamentably ill-governed. It makes no difference to any one having foreign protection, as to their personal safety, whether there be revolution or not. This white Americans and all Englishmen or anybody else have, but the free colored people of America. They have no protection anywhere.

Now this is a shame and a disgrace to the civilized world. But so it is, and, as Mr. Douglas would ask, "What are you going to do about it?"

I have no reason to doubt the sincerity of such eminent persons as have proposed to acknowledge the independence of these governments, form treaties therewith, and even to purchase territory and provide the means whereby a settlement could be established. I have rather much cause to believe the new government (that is to be) will give the subject earnest consideration. Nothing could be more just, and, as I believe, wise or popular. I know that such a measure would not be opposed by the people of the tropics, for there are many who entertain progressive ideas, and who have sympathies in common with Americans, who, the moment a protected settlement were established, would flock thither from the neighboring States and islands, and immediately swell the number of the original emigrants. I say I know this, because so many have said so, among whom could be mentioned English and American families, white and colored. But it pains me to say, the truth is, unless this protection could be given, or unless a sufficient number could emigrate (which they are not able to do) to protect themselves, none of these States seem to be in a sufficiently reliable condition to prevent such a movement from being a matter of great risk.

I have shown, I think, which was the object of this visit, what might be accomplished provided the government should provide means, never so small, towards the furtherance of such a movement.

It is the only way by which a colony to any extent could be permanently established, which would give tone and stability to the government there, and turn the important commerce of the tropics in this direction. There are now probably ten European vessels in the harbor[s] of Spanish America, but especially of Dominicana, where there is one belonging to the United States, although the latter is the natural market, from which they receive entirely their flour and salted pork. (Merchants of Cincinnati will appreciate this.)

I presume it would be difficult to find an American merchant in any of the Spanish States, who had not succeeded in making a fortune by the great advantages of trade in mahogany, dye-woods, hides, and tobacco, almost immediately after commencing business, but who has not as invariably lost it, in whole or in part, by the depression of currency in consequence of the momentary revolutions.

How grandly would both these and *those* States "loom up in the eyes of the world," if, abandoning that policy which makes them the indiscriminate oppressors of the weak, the American people should set themselves at work through their new administration, to secure by this means the commerce of those countries; give them peace, and forever wipe out the stain which Walker has cast upon the very name of all who boast themselves citizens of this republic. Such a measure would in some degree recompense the colored race for the services they have rendered to the government, the fruits of which they have not been permitted to enjoy; would make this great nation less obnoxious to the weak; lay the foundation of a future empire; and cause those lovely regions to bloom with industry and skill as they now bloom with eternal verdure.

Appendix

The Anglo-African Empire

(FROM THE ANGLO-AFRICAN MAGAZINE)

"Do these things mean nothing? What the tender and poetic youth dreams to-day and conjures up with inarticulate speech, is to-morrow the vociferated result of public opinion, and the day after is the charter of nations."—*Phillips*.

The stars of the tropics are the guiding stars of the age. The sympathy of the world is with the South, and the tendencies of things are southward. The controlling influence of the great commercial staple of our Southern States, the growing demand for the productions of the tropics, the discovery of gold toward the torrid zone, and a consequent want of labor in that direction, indicate firmly the force of these assertions. Other causes, apparently indirect or yet apparently opposed, such as the disappearance of slavery from Maine to Maryland, and the rapidity with which the slaves are hurried further south, might be cited on the one hand; and on the other the filibustering propensities of Southern fire-eaters as the unerring and immutable laws of destiny, guided by an all-wise and overruling Providence. "The coral zoöphite does not know that while it builds itself a house it also creates an island for the world;" and the master, as he pays the passage of his slave from the more Northern slave States to New Mexico, is but the rude agent of a superior power, urging him to more inviting fields for enterprise, and for his higher and more responsible duties as a freeman.

Reforms do not go backwards, nor filibustering

northwards, and "nothing is more certain than that the slaves are to be free;" but the problem as to what position they are to sustain as freemen is but little thought of, and, of course, less understood. It is true some suggestions have been offered on this subject, foremost among which stands that of Mr. Helper,* as the most absurd and ridiculous. It did not occur to Mr. Helper, when he suggested the broad idea of chartering all the vessels lying around loose for the huddling together of the blacks after emancipation and shipping them off to Africa,—it did not occur to him that they were men, and might not wish to go; at least it did not occur to him that they were *men*. So I make the suggestion for his benefit, and for the benefit of those who may come after him, this being a question not to be settled by arbitrary means, but by means which shall meet the approbation of all parties concerned, nor yet forgetting that at the head of these parties stands Him whose name is not to be mentioned without reverence.

Whence comes the colored people's instinctive horror of colonization in Africa? Colonizationists say they can not account for it, since Africa is their fatherland. But if this were any argument, I could account for it by the simple affirmation that it is not their fatherland. The truth is, "Time has shown that the causes which have produced races never to improve Africa, but to abandon it, and give their vigor and derive their strength from other climes, is not to be reversed by the best efforts of the best men." Besides this, charity begins at home. Allowing that the colonizationists, by sending a few handfuls of colored men to Africa, may plant the germ of civilization there, that the seed may spread or the fire may flame until the whole continent becomes illumi-

---

* Hinton Rowan Helper, *The Impending Crisis of the South: How To Meet It* (New York: A. B. Burdick, 1860). First published in 1857. Helper's antislavery views endeared him to the Republicans, but his attitude toward the Negro left much to be desired. The offending passage referred to above is found on page 183. H. H. B.

nated with Christian love, and her sons stand forth
regenerated and redeemed from the dark superstition
that enthralled them. Then what? It is a great deal, and a
great deal more than we can hope for, and a hero is he
who will sacrifice his life in making the attempt to bring
about such a magnificent result; but in doing this very
little will be accomplished for the millions who remain,
increasing, on this continent.

Nevertheless, there is a growing disposition among
colored men of thought to abandon that policy which
teaches them to cling to the skirts of the white people for
support, and to emigrate to Africa, Hayti, or wherever
else they may expect to better their condition; and it is
encouraging to know that the time is at hand when men
can speak their convictions on this subject without being
made the victims of il[l]iterate abuse and indiscriminate
denunciation, all of which is the natural result of more
general information, and which will lead to the discovery
at last of what is to be the final purpose of American
slavery—the destiny of the colored race after slavery shall
be abolished.

The history of Hayti and Jamaica, and of the American tropics generally, indicates the propagation of the
colored race, exclusive of whites or blacks. (This is simply calling things by their right names, for which the com-
piler of these facts expects to be made the most popular
writer of the age, of being highly flattered, infinitely
abused, feared, hated, and all that attends the discovery
of truth generally.) Throughout the West Indies, with
the single exception of Cuba, the whites have been unable to keep up their numbers, and in that instance only
by a recent flood of immigration on a large scale from
Europe. The colored race, on the contrary, is perfectly
well adapted to this region, and luxuriates in it; and it is
only through their agency that some small portion of
the torrid zone has been brought within the circle of
civilized industry. I have said their history would prove
this.

When discovered by the Spaniards these islands were inhabited by a colored people not unlike our Indians. Their homes were invaded; they were reduced to a state of miserable vassalage, and the proud Caucasian stalked about, the conquerer of every spot of earth his avarice or cupidity desired. The natives, unable to endure the persecutions to which they were subjected, withered and fell like the autumn leaves, and Africa became the hunting-ground of the slave pirate for hardier and more enduring slaves.

Africa became their hunting-ground, and quiet villages were startled in the dead of night to behold their huts in flames, and to hear the shrieks of their fellow-men and fellow-women, who were being torn away from their native homes as victims for the slave-ship, there to suffer all the tortures of the yoke and the branding-iron, and finally to be landed, if at all, on the American coast, with no other prospect than that of a life-bondage spread out before them. This state of wickedness continued, so far as England was concerned, until its glaring outrages challenged the attention of the British realm, and until the Parliament of England passed an act declaring all British subjects should be free;—"An act of legislation which, for justice and magnanimity, stands unrivalled in the annals of the world, and which will be the glory of England and the admiration of posterity when her proudest military and naval achievements shall have faded from the recollection of mankind;" an act of legislation which restored the liberties of eight hundred thousand of our fellow-men, *and left them in possession of superior claims and circumstances to those from which they had been originally removed,* (because, undoubtedly, the chances of any free man are better upon this continent than in Africa.)

Then came a series of American slanders: "Jamaica was ruined;" "the negro unfit for freedom;" and the downfall of prosperity and the loss of trade were everywhere said to be inevitable.

But the negro and his descendants are proof against slander and against the New York Herald, which terms are soon to be synonymous. Jamaica was not ruined: but, while these complaints were raised against her population, 40,000 land patents, varying from ten to one hundred acres each, were being taken up in a single year! Lands having been provided and schools introduced, happiness began to smile, prosperity reäppeared, and the whole country was redeemed from what had been a field of terror to what promises to become the very garden of the Western world.

This is said to be an axiom of political philosophy upon which it is safe to rely: *For any people to maintain their rights, they must constitute an essential part of the ruling element of the country in which they live.* The whites of the tropics are but few in number. They have heretofore sustained themselves by their superior wealth and intelligence. But, as fast as the colored people rise in this respect, their white rulers are pushed aside to make way for officers of their own race. This is perfectly natural. When a colony of Norwegians come over from Norway and settle a county in Wisconsin, do they elect a Yankee to represent them? Norwegians elect Norwegians, Germans elect Germans, and colored men elect colored men, whenever they have the opportunity.

Even now a large majority of the subordinate officers of Jamaica, I understand, are colored men. The Parliament is about equally divided, and the Attorney-General and Emigration Agent-General are colored men; and it is fair to assume, within a few years of the date of this paper, there will not be a single white man throughout the West Indies occupying a position within the gift of the people.

A retired merchant of Philadelphia, a man of large thought and liberal views, having an experience of fifteen or twenty years' residence in Hayti, in reply to certain letters asking for information and advice respecting the subject now under consideration, published a pamphlet in which he says: "There is a long view as well as a short view to be taken of every great question which bears upon human progress; but we are often unable or unwilling to take the former, until some time after a question is settled.

" 'Manifest destiny' has been, for some years, a familiar and accepted phrase in the mouths of our politicians, and each class suggests a plan for carrying it out in accordance with its own specific interests, or some preconceived theory. The pro-slavery adventurer may yet gain a footing in Central America, but it will not be to establish slavery. Slavery once abolished, has never been reëstablished in the same place, in America, except in one instance—that of the smaller French colonies, now again free. The vain effort to reënslave St. Domingo cost the French forty thousand men. The free negro, that nothing else can arouse, will fight against the replacement of the yoke which he has once thrown off; and the number of these in Central America is sufficient to prove a stumbling-block if not a barrier to its return. To reëstablish slavery permanently, where it has once been abolished, is to swin against the great moral current of the age.

"We can acknowledge to-day that the persecution of the Puritans by Laud and his predecessors, only intended, as it was, to produce conformity to the Church, really produced New England. And we can now see that the obstinacy of George the Third was as much a cause of the Declaration of Independence, at the time it was made, as the perseverance of John Adams,—the one being the necessary counterpart of the other, the two together forming the entire implement which clipped the tie. Now if we can make the above admissions in respect to these, the two greatest settled questions of modern times, without excusing either persecution or obstinacy in wrong, but keeping steadily in view that every man is responsible for the motives which govern his conduct, be the result of that conduct what it may, why should we not begin to look at this, the third great question of the same class, still *un*settled, from the same point of view?

"If, then, I were asked what was probably the final purpose of negro slavery, I should answer—To furnish the basis of a free population for the tropics of America.

"I believe that the Anglo-Americans, with the Africans, whom a part of the former now hold in bondage, will one day unite to form this race for the tropics, with or without combination with the races already there. But whether the African quota of it shall be transferred thither by convulsive or organized movements—or be gradually thinned out from their present abode, as from a great nursery, by directed but spontaneous transition— or retire, by degrees, with the 'poor whites,' before the peaceful encroachments of robust Northern labor, it would be useless now to conjecture. It is enough now to know that labor, like capital, goes in the end to the place where it is most wanted; and that labor, free from the destructive element of caste, has been, and still is, the great desideratum of the tropics, as it is of all other places which do not already possess it. I have already spoken of the presumed ability of the Southern States to spare this kind of labor. Should there, however, prove to be any part of the Union where the climate or the culture really requires the labor of the black man, then there he will remain, and eventually be absorbed by the dominant race; and from that point the complexion of our population will begin to shade off into that of the dark belt of Anglo-Africans, which will then extend across the northern tropics.

"I know that most of our Northern people, while they demand, in the strongest terms, all the rights of man for the negro or mulatto, are unable to eradicate from their minds a deeply-grounded prejudice against his person. In spite of themselves, they shrink from the thought of an amalgamation such as the foregoing observations imply. But these friends are not aware how quickly this prejudice begins to melt away as soon as one has entered any part of the tropics where the African race is in the ascendant, or where people of colored blood have attained to such social consideration as to make themselves respected. I suppose no Northern man ever forgets the occasion when, for the first time, he arrives at such a place, and the colored merchant to whom he is addressed comes forward, with the self-possession which attends self-respect, and offers him his hand. He begins to be healed of his prejudice from that hour."

I am also aware that the notion prevails generally in the United States that the mulatto has no vitality of race; that after three or four generations he dies out. This idea, I believe, finds its strongest advocates among the slaveholders and the readers of De Bow's "Review," and possibly it may be correct when applied to the colder latitudes; but I have no reason to think it is so in or near the tropics. Moreau de St. Méry, in his minute, "Description of the French part of St. Domingo,"* says, with respect to the vitality of the mulatto, which term includes all persons of color, however slight, of mixed European and African descent: "Of all the combinations of white and black, the mulatto unites the most physical advantages. It is he who derives the strongest constitution from these crossings of race, and who is the best suited to the climate of St. Domingo. To the strength and soberness of the negro he adds the grace of form and intelligence of the whites, and of all the human beings of St. Domingo he is the longest lived. . . . I have already said

---

* The French title: *Description Topographique, Physique, Civile, Politique et Historique de la Partie Française de l'Isle Saint Dominique.* . . . (2 vols.; Philadelphia, Chez l'auteur; Paris, Chez Dupont, 1797–98). H. H. B.

they are well made and very intelligent; but they are as much given to idleness and love of repose as the negro.

Hermann Burmeister, Professor of Zoölogy in the University of Halle, who spent fourteen months, in 1850–51, in studying at Brazil the "Comparative Anatomy and Physiology of the American Negro," speaks thus of the Brazilian mulatto: "The greatest number of the colored inhabitants of Brazil are of the negro and European races, called mulattoes. It may be asserted that the inferior classes of the free population are composed of such. If ever there should be a republic, such as exists in the United States of America, as it is the aim of a numerous party in Brazil to establish, the whole class of artisans would doubtless consist of a colored population. * * * Already in every village and town the mulattoes are in the ascendant, and the traveller comes in contact with more of them than of whites." There is nothing in these extracts, or in the essay from which they are taken, to indicate that the Brazilian mulatto is dying out. These are the observations of a patient investigator and man of science, and they have the more value, inasmuch as they were not set down to support any particular theory. The Professor speaks elsewhere in high but qualified terms of the moral and intellectual qualities of the mulatto, coming to conclusions similar to those of Moreau de St. Méry, except that he does not accuse them of indolence.

The author* of "Remarks on Hayti and the Mulatto," whose experience as a merchant I have mentioned, further says:

"This race, if on the white side it derives its blood from either the English or French stock, possesses within itself a combination of all the mental and physical qualities necessary to form a civilized and progressive popula-

---

* Harris does not identify this author other than to indicate (p. 168) that he is a retired merchant of Philadelphia who had spent fifteen or twenty years in Haiti. H. H. B.

tion for the tropics, *and it is the only race yet found of which this can be said."*

"I have no desire to undervalue the blacks of Hayti. I have found many shrewd, worthy, and intelligent men among them; and the country, it is well known, has produced several black men of a high order of talent; but these have been exceptional cases, like the King Philips, Hendricks, Tecumsehs, and Red Jackets of our North American Indians. As a race, they do not get on. *The same may be said of every other original race.* The blacks form no exception to the well-known law, that culture and advancement in man are the result of a combination of races."

I have no desire to retain, by the republishing of the above extracts, the appellation of "Defender of the Mulattoes;" but have inserted them here, that they may not be misunderstood. All I have to say is, that I believe it would be actually more proper, numerically speaking, to call at least the free persons of African descent in America, *colored* or mulattoes, rather than negroes. Yet, how often do we hear respectable men of all parties, talk the "Negro nationalities," and regarding the two races as "two negative poles mutually repelling each other," leaving no middle ground for the great mass of the colored people or mulattoes, whom, as some say, "God did not make." Instead of such impiety, and in place of sending one-half of the colored people to establish black nationalities in Africa, leaving the other half to be absorbed by the whites, I think it is much more liberal to regard them as one people, the political destiny of whom is unknown, or at best but begun to be discerned. To divide the colored people at this late day by any such process, would seem to me *like splitting a child in twain,* in order to give one half to its mother and the other to its father. *I go for a colored nationality,* that shall divide the continent with the whites, and the two empires being known respectively as Anglo-American and Anglo-African.

In conclusion, I desire to return my thanks for the complimentary manner in which the preceding communications have been received; and I would fain hope they might be as favorably regarded now that they are presented in this present form.

How proudly will the colored race honor that day, when, abandoning a policy which teaches them to cling to the skirts of the white people for support, they shall set themselves zealously at work to create a position of their own—an empire which shall challenge the admiration of the world, rivalling the glory of their historic ancestors, whose undying fame was chronicled by the everlasting pyramids at the dawn of civilization upon mankind.

> "Hope of the world! *the rising race*
> May heaven with fostering love embrace;
> And, turning to a whiter page,
> Commence with them *a better age;*
> An age of light and joy, which we,
> Alas! in prospect only see."

OPINIONS OF DISTINGUISHED STATESMEN AND PHILANTHROPISTS

"My proposition is simply to provide for the peaceful emigration of all those free colored persons of African descent who may desire so to emigrate to some place in Central or South America. . . . I believe the time has ripened for the execution of the plan originated by Jefferson in his day, agreed in by Madison and Monroe and all the earlier and better statesmen of the Republic, both North and South.—*Speech of Senator Doolittle.*

"Instead, therefore, of being an expense to the nation, the foundation of such a colony would be the grandest commercial enterprise of the age. . . . .
"Are the young merchants of Boston and of America indifferent to an enterprise which would give to our com-

merce, without a rival, such an empire as that to which I have pointed?—an empire not to be won by cruelty and conquest, but by peaceful and benignant means, and by imparting to others the inestimable blessings of liberty which we enjoy, and removing from our midst the only cause which threatens the prosperity and stability of the Union . . ."—*Speech of Hon. F. P. Blair, Boston.*

"It is my intention to use every effort to give practical effect to the propositions submitted to Congress, and I believe that the colored people themselves can give very efficient aid in the matter. If they will only let it be known that they approve, and are themselves willing to act upon the proposition, it will give it a great impulse."—*Hon. F. P. Blair— Letter to J. D. Harris.*

"The only mode in which we can relieve our country, relieve the blacks and whites, and provide separate homes for them, is by some scheme *which will meet the approbation of both—one which the parties themselves will execute.*"—*Hon. Preston King.*

"Among all feasible things, there is nothing that in my judgment would so much promote a peaceful abolition of slavery as your son's plan."—*Hon. Gerrit Smith to F. P. Blair, Sen.*

"The feeling of the free blacks in relation to African colonization is no criterion by which to judge of the success of American intertropical emigration. . . . I am confident that with proper inducements to be held out before them in regard to security of liberty and property, and prospects for well-doing, I could muster two hundred emigrant families or about one thousand colored persons annually for the next five years of the very best class for colonial settlement and industry, from various parts of the United States and Canada, who would gladly embark for homes in our American tropics."—*Rev. J. T. Holly.*

To the above might be added the views and opinions of many of the most eminent men in Ohio, Missouri, Illinois, Maryland, and other States, among them the Hon. Mr. Bates, and Sam'l T. Glover, Esq., of St. Louis. But none seem more appropriate to close this volume than the following from the Rev. Dr. Duffield, of Detroit.

Detroit, Feb. 18, 1860

DEAR BRO. KENDALL:—

Allow me to commend to your attention the object in which Mr. Harris has embarked. I think very favorably of it on various grounds, but regard it as especially indicative of God's providential designs in relation to the introduction of the gospel into that portion of our American continent which has attracted our attention, and which led yourself with me to memorialize the General Assembly on the subject of commencing a system of missions in Mexico, Central and Southern America. I had intended writing to you on the subject with a view to the prosecution of the matter of our memorial next spring, when the Assembly meets at Pittsburg. I know not, nor can I learn, what has been done in pursuance of the action of the last General Assembly. The whole matter as reported I failed to understand, and have since had no light shed upon the subject. May not this movement prove an occasion, if not of connection to the mission, of bespeaking a deeper interest in behalf of our benighted populations of Central and Southern America than has yet been felt by and in our country. . . .

Truly Yours,

GEO. DUFFIELD

REV. DR. KENDALL, of Pittsburg, Pa.